PSALMING THE BLUES

At the Intersection of Pain and Praise

A SEVEN-WEEK STUDY WITH

Dr. Tony W. Cartledge

THE *Nurturing* FAITH™

BIBLE STUDY SERIES

© 2015
Published in the United States by Nurturing Faith Inc., Macon GA,
www.nurturingfaith.net.

Library of Congress Cataloging-in-Publication Data is available.

ISBN 978-1-938514-76-0

*Unless otherwise indicated, scripture quotations are taken from
the New Revised Version of the Bible.*

Cover photo by John D. Pierce
The Western Wall in the Old City of Jerusalem on a rainy morning

Also available in

THE *Nurturing*
FA⊤TH™
BIBLE STUDY SERIES

A Place for Praise:
Ancient Psalms for Modern Times

An eight-week study with Dr. Tony W. Cartledge

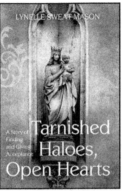

CONTENTS

ABBREVIATONS

ESV   English Standard Version

KJV   King James Version

HCSB   Holman Christian Standard Bible

NET   New English Translation (also known as the NETBible)

LXX   Septuagint, an early Greek translation of the Old Testament

MT   Masoretic Text, the "standard" Hebrew text of the Old Testament

NASB   New American Standard Bible, 1977 edition

NAS95   New American Standard Bible, 1995 edition

NIV   New International Version, 1984 edition

NIV11   New International Version, 2011 edition

NRSV   New Revised Standard Version

PREFACE

Bible study is a discipline that calls for the engagement of both hearts and minds. The Nurturing Faith Bible Study Series is designed to focus attention on biblical texts that expand the mind and enrich the heart.

Dr. Tony Cartledge brings the insights of a scholar, the heart of a pastor, and the communication skills of a seasoned writer and editor to this important task. With careful scholarship he guides learners to a clearer understanding of the context—language, culture, and setting—in which the biblical accounts occurred.

Then the important question is considered, "How do these ancient words speak to us as people of faith today?" Truth—not bound by time and culture—awaits those who are willing to explore, contemplate, and apply these biblical treasures.

Bible study deserves the best of both hearts and minds. So as a distinguishing mark, the Nurturing Faith Bible Study Series does not attempt to "dumb down" the lessons or to ignore the challenges of serious inquiry.

Therefore, each lesson contains "The Hardest Question" in which Dr. Cartledge both raises and responds to such challenges in understanding and applying the biblical revelation to today's living.

An honest wrangling with the biblical text—while guided by God's Spirit—can produce clearer understanding and stronger commitments. Such Bible study will indeed nurture one's faith.

The Bible is a compilation of sacred literature—diverse in style and genre. For example, these lessons from the Psalms explore the unique characteristics of Hebrew poetry.

Life is full of joy, yet not all of life is joyful. The question to be faced is not whether we will experience sadness and grief but where we will turn in such times. These insightful and inspiring lessons from selected psalms build trust and hope in the promises of God that have sustained generations.

Modern challenges often provide age-old feelings of loss, insecurity, and hopelessness. These honest, prayerful, poetic words of the psalmist, however, lead to places where life is sustained and the future can be faced with renewed faith. May your study of these psalms bring much insight and hope.

John D. Pierce, Publisher
Nurturing Faith, Inc.

This volume in the Nurturing Faith Bible Study Series is made possible
through a generous gift from Bob and Pat Barker and the Bob Barker Company
of Fuquay-Varina, North Carolina.

***

Nurturing Faith seeks sponsors for future volumes in this Bible study series.
To inquire, please contact office@nurturingfaith.net.

PSALMS, THEN AND NOW

INTRODUCTION TO HEBREW POETRY

We can't begin to appreciate the psalms unless we recognize that they were written as poetry, with many of them intended for singing as well as reading or reciting. One can enjoy the psalms and profit from reading them without knowing a thing about Hebrew poetry, but learning a few characteristic nuances can enhance both our appreciation and knowledge of the psalms.

Hebrew poetry is both like and unlike its English counterpart. To begin, with the exception of English free verse, both Hebrew and English poets speak in related phrases designed to carry a thought forward in lyrical fashion, generally following a detectable rhythm, or meter.

When we speak of meter, we think of **rhythm**, a pattern of beats that repeat. For example, we're familiar with these lines:

> 'Twas the night before Christmas, when all through the house
> Not a creature was stirring, not even a mouse.

These verses are written in a meter called "anapestic tetrameter," in which each line contains four units, each of which includes two weak beats and a strong one.

That meter was a favorite of another popular poet, as well:

> The sun did not shine, it was too wet to play,
> So we sat in the house all that cold cold wet day.[1]

We notice a clear pattern of beats, in which both accented and unaccented syllables play a role. We also hear a system of rhyme, with similar sounds occurring in a predictable pattern. In this case, the pattern is two unaccented syllables followed by an accented syllable.

In Hebrew poetry, the beat consists only of accented syllables, and the accented syllables are always on the important words. The neat interlude of the same number of unaccented syllables is not a primary characteristic, however. Sometimes a meter is generally recognizable (e.g. 3:3, 3:2), but the concept of "rhythm" in English and Hebrew poetry is somewhat different.

A second thing we generally associate with poetry is the concept of **rhyme**. Again, with the exception of free verse, we expect an arrangement in which patterns of lines end with the same sound.

Perhaps the shortest example of poetic rhyme is this one by e.e. cummings, titled "Fleas."

> Adam
> had 'em

Or consider Robert Frost's "The Road Not Taken," which begins like this:

> Two roads diverged in a yellow wood
> And sorry I could not travel both
> And be one traveler, long I stood
> And looked down one as far as I could
> To where it bent in the undergrowth.

Here, Frost uses a rhyming pattern of a-b-a-a-b.

Or consider this example of a limerick, attributed to Oliver Wendell Holmes, which has an a-a-b-b-a pattern:

> God's plan made a hopeful beginning,
> But Man spoilt his chances by sinning.
>> We trust that the story
>> Will end in great glory,
> But at present the other side's winning.

Rhyme is important to much English poetry, but is rare in Hebrew poetry. The latter rarely repeats sounds, but that does not mean it is not interested in repetition. In fact, Hebrew poetry is all about repetition, with its primary characteristic being a repetition of thoughts: its "rhyme" is one of sense rather than sound.

The basic unit of Hebrew verse is a couplet (also called a "bicola") in which the second line is roughly **parallel** to the first. Since the groundbreaking study of Bishop Robert Lowth,[2] scholars have recognized several variations in the pattern, but all of them in some way involve parallelism.

In *The Art of Biblical Poetry*, Robert Alter argues that the primary purpose of parallelism in all of its forms is for following lines to intensify the previous ones. Thus, he describes all types of parallelism as "structures of intensification."[3]

The easiest type of parallelism to recognize and understand is generally called **synonymous parallelism.** In it, the second line repeats the sense of the first line, but in different words. For example, consider Ps. 2:1:

Why do the nations conspire,
And the peoples plot in vain?

The word translated as "peoples" can describe an ethnic or political unit, so the conspiracy of nations and the peoples' plotting state the same thought.

Antithetic parellelism reinforces the first line from a contrary perspective— it gets the same idea across by stating something that sounds like the opposite. Here's an example from Ps. 37:9:

For the wicked shall be cut off:
But those who wait for the Lord shall possess the land.

These lines make the same point from different perspectives: The removal of the wicked from the land takes place in tandem with the installation of the righteous in their place.

A third type of parallelism is one in which the second line advances or intensifies the thought of the first line in a way that is neither synonymous nor antithetical. This is often called **synthetic** or **formal parallelism.**

Consider Isaiah's prayer (Isa. 64:1):

Oh, that you would rend the heavens and come down,
That the mountains would tremble before you!

These lines do not repeat the same thought, but the second line suggests the effect of the first: God's ripping of the heavens would cause the mountains to tremble.

Couplets are most common in Hebrew poetry, but triplets or tricola also appear, as in Job 3:5, where Job utters a triple curse on the day of his birth, repeating the same general thought in three different ways:

Let gloom and deep darkness claim it.
Let clouds settle upon it;
let the blackness of the day terrify it.

As in English, Hebrew poetry is particularly well suited for the expression of both pain and praise, for complaint and questions, for accusations and response. It served well the prophets who pronounced judgment and hope, for the psalmists who offered praise and lament, for the wisdom teachers who spoke in both aphorisms and deep questions.

INTRODUCTION TO THE BOOK OF PSALMS

The book of Psalms served as a repository of Israel's favorite hymns, both of praise and lament. We should be aware that it is not the only source of psalms, for they can also be found in narrative, prophetic, and wisdom books.

The Hebrew title of the book is *tehillim*, the plural form of a word meaning "song of praise" or "hymn."

The English name of the book comes from the Septuagint (LXX) title, *Psalmoi*, which is a translation of the Hebrew word *mizmor*, which appears 57 times as the title for a psalm. *Mizmor* means "song," generally of the type that may be accompanied by stringed instruments. The Greek word *psalterion* was also used in reference to psalms, which is why you sometimes hear the book referred to as "the Psalter."

As we have noted, the psalms—many of them, at least—were not just poems, but songs. Many of the psalms contain superscriptions that indicate the name of a tune, or some sort of instruction for the worship leader.

The psalms were also prayers, and so can be referred to by the Hebrew word *tephillot*, as at the end of Psalm 72, where it says "The prayers of David son of Jesse are ended."

Arrangement

The book of Psalms contains 150 psalms divided into five sections:

Book 1: 1-41
Book 2: 42-72
Book 3: 73-89
Book 4: 90-10
Book 5: 107-150

The division is mostly arbitrary except that the second section contains most of the "Elohistic Psalter," which stretches from 42-83 and is distinguished by the use of *Elohim* as the name for God. Some of these psalms appear twice in the psalter, employing *Elohim* in one place and *Yahweh* in another (Psalms 14 and 53 or Pss. 40:13-17 and 70). The division into five sections was probably done as an intentional parallel to the five books of the Torah.

We note that the numbering of the psalms is different in Protestant and Catholic Bibles, because Protestant Bibles are based on the Hebrew divisions, and

Catholic/Orthodox Bibles are based on divisions found in the Greek and Latin translations. To cite one example among several, Psalms 9 and 10 are separate in Hebrew, but one psalm in the Greek translation, abbreviated LXX. In addition, the LXX adds Psalm 151, which is not found in Protestant Bibles. The Syriac translation contains 155 psalms, some of which have also been found in texts at Qumran.

Authorship

Who wrote the psalms? Many people consider David, "the sweet psalmist of Israel" (2 Sam. 23:21, KJV), to be the author. There is indeed a tradition that David wrote many of the psalms, but the Bible makes no claim that he wrote them all. Texts such as 1 Chronicles 16, 2 Chron. 29:25-30, and Ezra 3:10 all associate David with the establishment of music as an integral part of Israel's worship, but he is properly seen as a patron and encourager of Israel's music and liturgy, not its sole author.

No less than 116 of the psalms have superscriptions in the Hebrew text, including 87 of the first 100. These are old traditions but not as old as the psalms themselves: they were added by later scribes and should not be considered a part of the original text. In some cases, what appears to be a superscription for one psalm may originally have been a postscript for the previous one. In the LXX, other superscriptions were added to all but the first two psalms. Some superscriptions appear to give instructions to the musicians or song leaders regarding which instruments or tune is to be played.

Among the superscriptions, 101 include attributive names, and *ledawid* appears 73 times. This doesn't necessarily mean "by David," however. The Hebrew prefix *l* more typically means "to" or "for," rather than "by." It could mean "of" in reference to a collection. Psalms are also attributed to (or for) Asaph (12), the sons of Korah (11), and Solomon (2), plus Heman, Ethan, and Moses (1 each).

Date

Determining a date for the writing of the Psalms is tricky business. Some psalms could be as old as two centuries before David and others may be as late as the fifth century, looking back after the exile. There is more evidence of early Hebrew than late.

The presence of the "Elohistic psalter" makes it clear that the psalms were rather fluid and subject to some changes as time went on. And, a few psalms appear in slightly different form in other parts of the Bible. Psalm 18, for example, also appears in 2 Samuel 22 as a song of David. Jer. 17:5-8 contains much of the same material found in Psalm 1, where it has been transformed into a song.

The appearance of an obvious wisdom teaching as the first psalm could suggest that the wisdom school had some influence on the final shape of the psalter.

Ancient Near Eastern Parallels

We should point out that psalms and hymns were not unique to Israel. Hymns of various sorts are known from Ugarit, Sumeria, Babylonia, and Egypt. It is often noted, for example, that Psalm 104 has some similarities to the Egyptian Hymn to Aten.

While space does not allow us to provide examples of other hymns from the ancient Near East, readers should be aware that hymnic prayers were not unique to Israel. Occasionally, we may note a similarity of expressions found in Hebrew psalms and poetry from neighboring cultures.

General Characteristics, Theology

The psalms are not only to be understood as poetry, and as songs, but also as prayers. Most of them address either petitions or complaints to God. A few are addressed to other people, but in order to call upon them to celebrate God's power or to follow God's law.

Some of the psalms are clearly cultic and designed for official occasions, even something like the coronation of a king. Others appear to be very personal, such as the penitent Psalm 51.

Although themes such as wisdom, covenant, repentance, and Torah are often found in the psalms, the central theological theme is the presence of God—either giving thanks for God's presence or pleading for God's presence.

Setting/Function

What was the function of the psalms in Israel? When and where and how were they used?

We presume that they eventually wound up in Jerusalem and were used in cultic ceremonies through the temple, but some of them may have originated in other settings. For example, Psalm 74 speaks of an exilic setting after the destruction of the temple, and Psalm 81 may have originated in the Northern Kingdom (it speaks much of "Israel"). And, if Psalms 18 and 60 were not written prior to the establishment of the temple, they are designed to appear that way, as prayers of David when he was in a tight spot. A number of the psalms appear to have been composed for particular purposes on special days.

Priests, prophets, wisdom teachers, and other worshipers may have contributed psalms. The emphasis on David's role in promoting music may suggest that collections of psalms first began under David's sponsorship. Later, others were added, and they were reorganized.

Types of Psalms

Hermann Gunkel, the great German form critic, pioneered the application of form criticism to the psalms, and identified a variety of different types (*gattungen*) of psalms. Although our interpretation of a psalm is not limited by its primary type, it is helpful to compare a psalm with others of a similar type.

We can identify both major types of psalms, and varieties of related types within them. Sometimes a psalm will contain elements of multiple types. And, as one might expect, scholars do not always agree on what psalms belong to what type.

Hymns and psalms of praise constitute the largest category. About 74 of the 150 psalms focus on praise to God. They typically begin with a call to praise God, and then list reasons why one should offer praise, often concluding with a closing call to praise.

Laments make up the next group. About 56 psalms are of this type, most of them (40) being individual prayers of lamentation, the most frequent single type. These may spring from different contexts. They typically begin with a cry for hearing or expression of certainty that God will hear. They plead with God for deliverance, usually express trust that God will hear their prayer, and offer words of praise in advance of it actually happening. The lessons in this book are drawn from the psalms of lament.

Royal psalms relate directly to the Davidic dynasty and its rule in Jerusalem. These include Psalms 2, 18, 20, 21, 45, 72, 89, 101, 110, 132, and 144.

Wisdom psalms reflect Israel's wisdom traditions. These include Psalms 1, 37, 49, 73, 112, 119, 127, 128, and 133.

With this great variety of material, the Psalms have something for everyone. psalms for happy days and sad days, confident days and questioning days, days of celebration and days when it seems that God is hiding. As we read how Israel's poets testified of their encounters with God—especially in times of trial or sorrow—we find that we have not only gained knowledge of God, but also learned something about ourselves.

NOTES

[1] Dr. Seuss, *The Cat in the Hat* (Random House, 1957).

[2] *De sacra poesi Hebraeorum* (1753), refined by G. Buchanan Gray in *The Forms of Hebrew Poetry* (London: Hodder and Stoughton, 1915).

[3] Robert Alter, *The Art of Biblical Poetry* (New York: Basic Books, 1985), 88.

Psalm 23

TRUST ME

Even though I walk through the darkest valley,
I fear no evil;
for you are with me;
your rod and your staff—
they comfort me.
—Psalm 23:4

If you could choose a hymn to be sung at your funeral, what would it be? Many of us would choose a song of trust and testimony that speaks of what we believe God has done for us. Perhaps no hymn is more beloved, for those reasons, than "Amazing Grace."

Psalm 23 is the "Amazing Grace" of the Psalter. It speaks of the psalmist's trust and testimony, but it is also *our* story. Whether we find ourselves at rest beside still waters, following in the paths of righteousness, or struggling through valleys of deep shadow, this psalm has a word for us.

> ⛏ **This is a lament?** It may seem strange that the first lesson in a series on the "psalms of lament" would be the beloved 23rd psalm, which is hardly a lamentation. As we proceed, however, you will notice that most psalms of lament include strong affirmations of trust in God. The element of trust is so pervasive in the laments that many scholars consider psalms of trust, such as this one, to be a sub-category of the psalms of lament. While trust predominates in Psalm 23, the psalm recalls previous experiences with deep valleys and even the dark shadow of death. Thus, while specific laments are absent, painful memories lurk in the background. Trust has grown out of lament.

GOD AS SHEPHERD
(vv. 1-4)

⛏ God as shepherd in scripture: The biblical image of God as a shepherd is not limited to Psalm 23. Jacob's blessing of Joseph, from Gen. 49:24, speaks of God as "the Shepherd, the Stone of Israel."

Other psalms employed the image, too. In a deep lament, the author of Psalm 80 cries out "Oh give ear, Shepherd of Israel, Thou who dost lead Joseph like a flock ..." (v. 1). On a happier note, Ps. 100:3 declares "We are his people, and the sheep of his pasture."

Isaiah of the Exile chose the image of God as a shepherd to speak words of comfort to his lost companions, assuring them of God's coming redemption and future care: "Like a shepherd he will tend his flock, in his arm he will gather the lambs, and carry them in his bosom; he will gently lead the nursing ewes" (Isa. 40:11 [NASB]).

The portrait of God as shepherd finds completeness in the New Testament, where Jesus took it as his own: "I am the good shepherd; the good shepherd lays down his life for the sheep" (John 10:11). Peter would later refer to Christians as those who had "returned to the Shepherd and Guardian of your souls" (1 Pet. 2:25, cf. 5:4).

Israel's background as a nomadic people makes it only natural that a Hebrew poet would picture God as a shepherd. Employing such a metaphor identifies with the sheep and implies a willingness to follow the shepherd's leading. ⛏

In this relationship, the psalmist says, "I shall not want." This is not a promise that we will never want more than we have, but that we will not lack God's care. ⛏

The psalmist knew that we all have work to do, for God does not rain manna from heaven when there is grain in the field. Yet, he also knew it was God who brought the sun and the rain to bear upon the grain. The Good Shepherd's presence points us in ways that meet our physical, emotional, and spiritual needs. ⛏

But sheep need more than food and water. Left to their own in a lush pasture, sheep might eat far more than is good for their health, even as humans may confuse meeting basic needs with acquiring luxuries.

Smart shepherds periodically direct the animals to lie down and take time to chew their cud. This promotes complete digestion and is good for their health.

It would be stretching it to suggest that God brings disease or tragedy to "make us lie down" and take stock of our lives, but God can use both times of rest and difficult times to help us reflect on and "digest" what has been happening in our lives, making us stronger and better people. Wise believers take time to rest and ruminate on God's place in our lives.

⚓ **Yahweh:** The key to understanding the importance of this psalm is found in the first word: "Yahweh is my shepherd," the psalmist says (v. 1a). The Bible places great significance on names, and God revealed the name Yahweh to Israel.

The psalmist does not refer to God in abstract terminology such as "The Lord," as we often translate the name, but uses God's personal name because the psalm is about a personal relationship between the psalmist and God.

While scholars are divided on the Hebrew derivation of the name Yahweh (if, indeed, it is related to any other words at all), the most likely suggestion is that it comes from the causative form of the verb "to be." God is the author of all existence. As John I Durham used to describe God's explanation of the name to Moses, "I am the was is, the is is, and the will be is I am Mister Is!"

⚓ **Food and water:** The psalmist described various aspects of God's care, including the ability to access food and water. "He makes me to lie down in green pastures," the psalmist says. Fields of green are not always easy to find in the non-irrigated areas of Palestine. Because of the arid conditions, grass may grow only at certain times of the year, or at certain elevations. The shepherd's task in a nomadic society includes knowing when and where grass is growing in the territory he is allowed to use.

So it is that the shepherd awakens the sheep before daylight each morning, and leads them out to what the psalmist literally describes as "fields of grass." "Green pastures" expresses the same thought in more poetic language. Once in the fields, the shepherd keeps the sheep moving so they will not overgraze any one spot, for the pastures will be needed again.

Sheep, like humans, need water as well as food. When the dew is heavy, sheep don't need to drink, but as the day goes on, fresh water becomes essential. In the barren reaches of Palestine, water is as scarce as grass, and is sometimes found in fast-flowing streams. Since sheep are notoriously timid, running water makes them nervous. Sheep may refuse to drink from a moving stream, even if they are desperately thirsty. Because of this, the shepherd must lead the sheep "beside the still waters," literally, "beside waters of rest."

When the shepherd cannot find a pool or eddy where the water is quiet, he may build a temporary dam to create a pool of still water. Where surface water is not available, the shepherd resorts to deep wells, where he must work even harder to draw enough water for the sheep to drink.

⛏ **"Cast"-aways:** Stories of sheep becoming lost or falling into dangerous places are familiar. Less familiar is the phenomenon of becoming "cast." Sheep prefer to lie down in a shallow depression, because it is more comfortable. If a sheep is particularly fat or heavy with wool, it may accidentally roll onto its wide back, and not be able to get up. Sheep in this situation are said to be "cast," and can die unless the shepherd finds them and carefully returns them to an upright position.

God not only provides food, water, and guidance, but also "restores my soul," the psalmist said. The word for "restore" is an intensive form of the verb "to (re) turn," and it means "to bring back." The word translated as "soul" is the Hebrew *nephesh*, which speaks of one's whole life, both physical and spiritual.

Sheep are among the world's most stress-prone animals, often in need of reassurance and encouragement. When a shepherd scratches the animal or calls it by name, the sheep's sense of security and belonging increases. In such cases, the shepherd "refreshes the spirit" of the sheep.

In some cases, the shepherd must literally save the life of an animal, rescuing it from being lost, falling into danger, or rolling over and being "cast" so that it can't get up. ⛏

Christians have no difficulty in thinking of ways in which God "restores our soul" or "brings back our life." Christ, the good shepherd, saves us from those things that would "steal, and kill, and destroy" so that we "might have life, and have it to the full" (John 10:10).

Sheep, left to their own devices, will inevitably wander—as humans also do. Isaiah once declared: "All of us, like sheep, have gone astray, each of us has turned

⛏ **Rightness, and righteousness:** The word translated as "right" in v. 3 could mean either "rightness" or "righteousness." The main image is that of a shepherd leading the flock on the right or appropriate paths to get them where they need to go. The shepherd is careful to do this, not only for the sake of the sheep, but also for the sake of his own name and reputation. Who wants to be known as the shepherd who got lost?

When the application is made to persons, it is proper to think of both "right paths" and "righteous paths." As we follow his leading, the Good Shepherd will lead us in right paths—to the places we need to go, to the people we need to help. At the same time, the Lord leads us to walk righteously (though not self-righteously!). Those who follow Christ through prayer, Bible study, and a sense of openness to the Spirit's presence find that God provides guidance for both our direction and our behavior.

to his own way" (Isa. 53:6). Knowing that the sheep need guidance, the shepherd leads them "in the right paths." ✪

The Good Shepherd leads us properly "for his name's sake," because that reflects God's nature. Humans cannot walk rightly in their own strength any more than sheep can always choose the correct pathway home.

A notable shift takes place in v. 4. Instead of speaking *about* God as shepherd ("He leads me," "He restores my soul"), the psalmist begins speaking *to* God: "Even though I walk through the darkest valley, I fear no evil, for *you* are with me—*your* rod and *your* staff, they comfort me."

The author appears to know what a deep, dark valley looks like. This verse may be a personal testimony of bleak times he had known, and of the Good Shepherd's comforting presence.

We must be careful not to divorce v. 4 entirely from the reference to following right paths in v. 3b, however. We may stray into a valley of deep darkness, but the right path may also involve shadowy or dangerous places. ✪

When Middle Eastern shepherds take their sheep to the summer grazing lands, they often go into the mountains, and there are no mountains without valleys, places that may be deep in shadow and frequented by wild animals or thieves. We also will walk in deep, dark valleys—all of us. ✪

✪ **The dark valley:** Israeli tour guides often point to the deep Wadi Qelt—where St. George's Monastery perches on its steep side—as a locale that might have inspired the image of "the valley of the shadow of death."

✪ **Can we opt out?** Some translations begin v. 4 with "Even though I walk . . ." (NRSV, NASB), which seems to suggest that walking in dark valleys is only a possibility, to be experienced by the unfortunate. The text, however, is open to another translation, for the word *kî* can be rendered as "when" as well as "if."

"Even when I walk through the valley . . ." suggests more certainty, and is closer to our actual experience. None of us can avoid valleys altogether.

⛨ **The valley of the shadow of death:** The translation of this phrase has been the subject of much debate among scholars. The Hebrew expression uses the word for "valley" followed by a compound word that appears to be formed from the words for "shadow" and "death." The most apparent, most literal translation, then, is the familiar rendering of the King James Version, "valley of the shadow of death" (also NASB, RSV, NIV).

Other translators read the word as a poetic description of deep darkness. Thus, we have versions ranging from the mild "gloomy valley" (Jerusalem Bible) to "darkest valley" (NRSV) and "valley of deepest darkness" (NJPS, a modern Jewish version). Translators of the New English Bible found a way to include both thoughts with "a valley dark as death." None of them sound pleasant.

Some interpreters make a great deal of the word "through," as the psalmist said "Even though I walk *through* the darkest valley . . ." (NRSV). The prepositional prefix used can indeed mean "through," but it most commonly means "in" or "into." There will be at least one valley we will walk *into* but not out of. The psalmist is, after all, talking about "the valley of the shadow of death." ⛨

The important thing about this valley is not how deep or dark or dangerous it is. The significant thing is that in the midst of the dark valley, God is with us. "I fear no evil, for you are with me." This is a strong, intensive phrase in Hebrew, reflecting God's promises to the patriarchs. As Jacob undertook the dangerous journey to Haran, for example, Yahweh appeared to him and made this promise: "Know that I am with you and will keep you wherever you go . . ." (Gen. 28:15, cf. the promise to Isaac in Gen. 26:3).

There is great power in presence. The timorous sheep can feel safe, even in a dark and dangerous place, because the shepherd is near, and will not desert the flock.

For reflection: *Psalm 23 is written from the perspective of a cooperative sheep. Keeping in mind both vv. 3 and 4, think on this: If I am unwilling to follow on the paths of righteousness, can I expect the shepherd to be with me when I stumble into paths of darkness?*

Can you think of times when you have felt especially close to God? Did these occur more often in green pastures, or in dark valleys?

To describe his sense of security, the psalmist says "I will fear no evil." The psalm does not promise that we will face no harm in this life, only that we need not *fear* it. The Lord who is present with us has ultimate power over all that is evil.

The shepherd analogy concludes with a reference to two potent sticks that shepherds typically carried. The "rod" was a short club that could also be thrown to frighten away predators or to bring a straying sheep back into the safety of the group.

The "staff" calls to mind a tall walking stick the shepherd might lay against the side of a sheep to guide its direction, or use to scratch its stomach in a show of affection.

God's rod and staff call to mind discipline, protection, and guidance. The beauty of nature, the love of friends, and the touch of the Spirit all speak of God's presence.

GOD AS HOST
(vv. 5-6)

With v. 5, there is another dramatic shift. The author no longer speaks from the perspective of a sheep, but as a guest in God's house, where Yahweh is no longer the ideal shepherd, but the perfect host. Preparing a table, anointing with oil, and filling the cup are all clear images of a joyful meal in which the psalmist finds himself an honored guest at the Lord's table. ♦

The poet paints a remarkable picture. God has not just "set in order" a table before him, but has done so in the very presence of hostile opponents. While the image is different, the verse carries forward the same themes found in the previous verses: God provides not only food and rest, but also protection.

The joy of this special fellowship is indicated by the reference to anointing with scented oil, a ceremony used for the anointing of kings or the welcoming of honored visitors. The final picture also echoes the theme: The psalmist's joy, symbolized by an overflowing cup of wine, has filled him to the point of spiritual satiation. ♦

♦ **Table, or tablelands?:** Some interpreters ignore the shift from shepherd to host in vv. 5-6, stretching the language to retain the pastoral metaphor. Phillip Keller, for instance, speaks of the shepherd taking his sheep to the high "tablelands," where he "prepares the table" by removing poisonous weeds from the pasture. Furthermore, he explains "You anoint my head with oil" as a reference to the shepherd's provision of ointments to protect the sheep from flies and infections. This makes impressive devotional reading, but probably stretches and misses the point of the original text.[1]

For reflection: *Can you think of other biblical images in which God is pictured as a joyful host, and Christians are invited? Does your church set aside times for pure fun and rejoicing? Can you think of ways to help your church learn to celebrate?*

Having reflected on God's past provision and present fellowship, the psalmist turned toward the future, using an intriguing metaphor: the goodness and the steadfast love of God would "follow" him throughout his life.

This picture is comforting. Some interpreters like the impressive image of God going *before* the psalmist to the green pastures, walking *beside* him in the dark valley, and following *behind* him (in goodness and love) throughout life.

Another image is also appealing. The word translated "follow after me" derives from the verb that most commonly means "to pursue," or "to chase." God's dependable goodness and steadfast love not only follow us into the future, but also chase us into closer fellowship.

Some writers interpret "house of the Lord" as a strict reference to the temple, suggesting that the psalmist intends to establish his permanent residence on

🍶 **Oily hair:** "You anoint my head with oil" literally means "you make fat, with oil, my head"! Anointing oil was often scented (Exod. 25:6), and was used to denote the choice of a new king (1 Sam. 10:1, 16:13; Ps. 133:1-2) and to greet guests (Luke 7:46).

Oil is sometimes used in scripture as a symbol of joy. As Job recalled his days of blessing, he spoke of oil gushing from the rocks (Job 29:6), and when Isaiah proclaimed the Lord's coming deliverance, he spoke of how God would give the people of Israel "a garland instead of ashes, the oil of gladness instead of mourning . . ." (Isa. 61:3).

In praising the new king, one of the psalmists exulted: "God, your God, has anointed you with the oil of gladness beyond your companions" (Ps. 45:7, cf. Heb. 1:9). A hymn in praise of unity asserts "How very good and pleasant it is when kindred live together in unity! It is like precious oil on the head, running down upon the beard, on the beard of Aaron, running down over the collar of his robes" (Ps. 133:1-2, NRSV).

It is this image that the psalmist evokes when he speaks of sitting at God's table, being welcomed into God's extravagant hospitality with the anointing oil of gladness.

Mt. Zion. This view misses the point: The poet is not just talking about a place, but confidently expressing his hope of future fellowship with God, a fellowship based not on his own goodness but on the goodness and love of God.

This confidence in the future extends as far as the psalmist can imagine: forever (literally, "for the length of days").

Psalm 23 begins and ends on a note of confident joy in the presence of God. This joy is not fleeting or temporary, like a butterfly that we see and delight in for a short time. The joy of God's presence is always in pursuit of his people, and it lasts as long as time itself.

THE HARDEST QUESTION
What does it mean that God's "goodness and mercy shall follow me"?

God's "goodness" is here denoted by the very common word *tôv*. The term can be used in a variety of senses, from adjectives such as "good" and "beautiful" to the comparative "better" (as in Ps. 118:8-9), and the noun form "goodness." *Tôv* may have a qualitative sense (referring to that which is pleasant or of fine quality), or it may have a moral sense, denoting good as opposed to evil (Gen. 3:5, Amos 5:14).

God is good (Ps. 25:8, 34:8, 100:5; Mark 10:18), and creation reflects the divine goodness (Gen. 1:4, 10, 12, et. al.), including humankind (Gen. 1:31). The Lord continually blesses the earth with goodness (Ps. 73:1, 145:9), for which his people offer praise (Ps. 118:5, 135:3, 136:1).

As God is good, God's people are called to be good (Deut. 12:28). Throughout the "Deuteronomistic History" (Deuteronomy-2 Kings, with the exception of Ruth), Israel's fortunes rise and fall on the basis of whether the people and their leaders choose to obey God and do good, or to reject God's way and follow evil.

Wisdom literature such as the book of Proverbs uniformly upholds the virtue of goodness (Prov. 11:27), even as the prophets habitually exhort the people to do good, and not evil (Amos 5:14-15). At least one prophet took a stab at defining the goodness that is expected of God's people: "He has told you, O mortal, what is good; and what does the Lord require of you, but to do justice, and to love kindness, and to walk humbly with your God?" (Mic. 6:8, NRSV).

Living out the goodness of God is our goal, in a sense, but God's goodness is also a stimulus to better living. As a child is encouraged in good behavior by the kindness of her parents, so the goodness of God motivates people to *be* good and to *do* good, seeking God's presence day by day.

The word translated as "mercy" is *hesed*, a special word denoting a special kind of love, so rich in meaning that we have difficulty expressing it in one English word.

The basic meaning of *hesed* is "love," but there are also elements of "kindness," "mercy," and "loyalty." The KJV often translates with "mercy" or the compound term "lovingkindness," which sounds a bit archaic, but comes close to the intended meaning.

God declared God's nature to Moses with this term: "Yahweh, Yahweh, a god merciful and gracious, slow to anger, and abounding in steadfast love (*hesed*) and faithfulness, keeping steadfast love (*hesed*) for the thousandth generation, forgiving iniquity and transgression and sin. . ." (Exod. 34:6-7a, cf. Num. 14:8-9; Neh. 9:17; Ps. 103:8; Joel 2:13; Jon. 4:2).

Hesed, then, refers to the love of God in all its richness, a love that is steadfast and enduring. God's *hesed* is both constant (Ps. 42:8, 92:2) and eternal (1 Chron. 16:34, 41; Ps. 100:5, 106:1, 136).

In scripture, perhaps the clearest human picture of this faithful love is the prophet Hosea, who pursued his chosen Gomer with a love that was steadfast, despite her less-than-faithful response. "I will take you for my wife forever," he said. "I will take you for my wife in righteousness and in justice, in steadfast love (*hesed*), and in mercy (Hos. 2:19, NRSV [Heb. 2:21]).

Throughout the Old Testament, God pursues Israel with steadfast love, despite the people's unfaithfulness. In the New Testament, we see Jesus, who goes the final mile in demonstrating God's faithful love as he died on the cross. This demonstration of his love motivates us to love him in return: "We love him, because he first loved us" (1 John 4:19).

Like the psalmist, we are also pursued by the abundant goodness and the steadfast love of God. In the Old Testament, these terms are often combined in the writings of those who would offer praise to God: "Give thanks to the Lord, for he is good; for his steadfast love endures forever" (Ps. 106:1, 136:1, 1 Chron. 16:34, Jer. 33:11).

Because of love, God does not give up on us, but pursues us gently with blessings of goodness and the appeal of steadfast love. The poet recognizes that this is not a brief chase, but a life-long relationship. As long as he lives, wherever he goes, God's goodness and steadfast love will be close behind, tirelessly driving him more deeply into the joys of divine hospitality.

NOTE

[1]Phillip Keller, *A Shepherd Looks at Psalm 23* (Grand Rapids: Zondervan, 1970), 105-106, 114-19.

Psalm 25:1-10

HEALTHY REGRET

Do not remember the sins of my youth or my transgressions;
according to your steadfast love remember me
for your goodness' sake, O LORD!
—Psalm 25:7

Penitence. Contrition. Regret. Remorse. Sorrow. Self-reproach. Shame. Guilt. We don't like those words, do we? But we've all felt them, and for cause. We've disappointed God, disappointed others, and disappointed ourselves. We've made bad choices, taken wrong turns, and generally messed up.

We've sinned, to use a good biblical term. And, unless we're one of those very rare sociopaths who have no conscience, we've felt guilty. We've experienced shame.

♍ **Lament, or trust?:** Most scholars classify Psalm 25 as an "individual prayer of lament," but it differs in some ways from typical laments. Most psalms of lament arise from times of distress when the poet cries for deliverance from illness or from enemies. The distress in this psalm comes from the poet's personal failings and his desire to be forgiven, lest he be put to shame. Like many psalms of lament, it contains a strong element of trust that God will hear the prayer and act in mercy to deliver, vindicate, or forgive the petitioner.

Peter C. Craigie, who suggests that the psalm might better be classified as a "prayer of confidence," says this about trust: "He trusts because God is faithful as the God of the covenant promises; he trusts because those who have trusted in the past have experienced the presence and help of God . . . Trust, then, is neither naïve and misplaced confidence, nor is it self-confidence; it is a human response to God's self-revelation in covenant and in historical experience, both personal experience and that of the community."[1]

And we don't like it. We want to be forgiven—forgiven by those persons we've wronged, and if we have any religious compunction about us, forgiven by God, as well.

That's what Psalm 25 is about: a prayer for forgiveness, offered in trust to a gracious God. It is often read on the first Sunday of Lent, but self-reflection and penitence are appropriate at any time of the year. ♉

HEAR ME . . .
(vv. 1-3)

♉**Acrostic:** Psalm 25 is designed as an acrostic, one of eight such poems in the Psalms (9-10, 25, 34, 47, 111, 112, 119, 145). In Psalm 25, each two-line unit begins with a corresponding letter of the Hebrew alphabet (or "*alefbet*"), from the first letter, *alef*, to the last letter, *tau*.

Such careful construction gives evidence that the psalm is a literary creation rather than a spontaneous prayer, designed for use in worship or by anyone who felt the need of forgiveness.

The psalm's acrostic scheme would have made the poem easier for Hebrew speakers to memorize, but the artificial system works against the poet's ability to give the psalm clear structure. As a result, it wanders about from one theme to another and then back again. Fortunately, this does not prevent us from discerning three primary themes, all of which speak to the human proclivity to sin and the universal need for forgiveness.

Like several other psalms, Psalm 25 is an acrostic poem, written so that each couplet begins with a sequential letter of the Hebrew alphabet. ♉ And, like many psalms, this one begins with the Hebrew expression *ledawid*, which can mean "of David," "by David," or "to/for David." ♉

The psalmist seeks forgiveness, but offers no clue as to what sins he has committed. That works to the reader's advantage, for the unspoken nature of the psalmist's guilt makes it easier for us to apply his situation to our own lives—and all of us have sinned.

Have you ever "poured out your heart" to God? That's the sense of the psalmist's opening words, "To you, O LORD, I lift up my soul." The psalmist's use of God's covenant name "Yahweh" (LORD) reflects the intimate, personal nature of the prayer. The word translated as "soul" (*nefesh*) describes one's essential being, the source of life and identity. To lay bare our soul before God is to go as deep as we can go.

The psalmist can present himself to Yahweh so freely and deeply because he trusts God to hear his prayer and respond with care. Perhaps you have

♉ **By David, or for David?:** Contrary to popular belief, the opening words *ledawid* does not necessarily indicate that David wrote the psalm. Not only does the prefix *l* more commonly mean "for" or "to," but superscriptions such as this one were probably added as the psalms were being compiled into a scroll, long after the psalm itself gained popular usage.

had the experience of sharing deep thoughts or confessions with someone who didn't make much of an effort to understand. Worse, you may have trusted personal experiences to someone who went out and told other people what you had revealed in confidence. Instead of feeling comforted, you felt embarrassed or ashamed. Untrustworthy friends may let us down, but God can be trusted to hear and understand our innermost fears, thoughts, or confessions—even our doubts.

The psalmist appears to have sought some outward sign of divine favor that would silence the smug criticism of "enemies" who would find joy in his sorrow. The word for "put to shame" appears three times in vv. 2-3. The poet pleads that God would not bring shame to those who patiently trust ("wait") in God, but would humiliate those who are deceitful, or disloyal.

For reflection: *Do you think the psalmist had experienced hurt or embarrassment at the hands of someone he had trusted? Have you had that experience? More pointedly, have you ever been the person who betrayed another's trust and caused them pain? It's likely that we've all been on both sides of that divide. All of us could do with a good dose of divine guidance to help keep us on the right path.*

GUIDE ME . . .
(vv. 4-5)

The psalmist prayed for God's guidance in no less than four different ways, asking Yahweh to "make me to know your ways," to "teach me your paths," to "lead me in your truth," and, simply, to "teach me" (vv. 4-5a).

All four expressions acknowledge that the poet is not only willing but also anxious for God to teach him. "Your ways," "your paths," and "your truths" were favored terms among Israel's teachers of wisdom. These terms could refer to any commandments and laws to be found in biblical teaching, but go beyond that.

One could learn the commandments and the rules of community living by reading or listening to a teacher, but the psalmist seeks more. He longs for God's guidance as he deals with everyday situations or makes life decisions that aren't covered by written laws.

We are constantly faced with choices: where to attend college, what job to pursue, who (or whether) we will marry, whether we want to have or adopt children. We make daily choices about how we will spend our time, our money, and our energy. Do we run through these choices without a thought beyond our personal preferences, or do we stop to ask God's guidance? God may not care whether we have spaghetti or fish for dinner, but larger decisions or moral judgments call for deeper reflection. If we want our choices and our lives to honor God, and if we want to be known as upright and faithful people, we need to consider what God might have us do.

Those who teach that God has a specific plan mapped out for us overstate the case: Whether we work for company A or company B may not be of much divine consequence as long as we work faithfully and ethically. Whether we marry now, five years from now, or never may not concern God, but how we behave clearly does.

The point is, if we don't lay important decisions before God and remain open to whatever impressions God may lay upon our hearts or minds, we increase the chance of making a wrong turn.

This is not to suggest that we will get immediate answers. The psalmist expressed his trust in Yahweh as "the God of my salvation," for whom he was willing to "wait all day long" (v. 5b). As we read the psalm through the lens of the New Testament, we naturally think of God's salvation as being an eternal pardon through Jesus Christ. The psalmist's idea of "salvation," however, would have involved deliverance from some difficult situation or person.

Both acts of deliverance involve a change of course. We can't count on a heavenly voice or an angelic finger to point us in the right direction, but as our souls remain open to God's leadership, we are more likely to sense what path would be most pleasing to God—and thus most appropriate for us.

FORGIVE ME . . .
(vv. 6-7)

After humbly beseeching God to hear and to guide, the psalmist turns to a theme he will repeat in vv. 11 and 18: a plea for forgiveness. We do not know if he has any particular sin in mind. Indeed, his request that God not remember the sins and transgressions of his youth may suggest that he is no longer young, but looking back over his life and hoping God will overlook his sinful forays and remember his better days. ⬗

⚜ **Sins and transgressions:** In Hebrew, the first word of v. 7 is derived from a verb that means "to miss the mark" or "to stray." If the subject is an arrow, it means the archer missed the target. If the subject is life, it means the person has gone off the straight path and done wrong. Its typical translation, as here, is "to sin."

The word translated as "transgressions" comes from a verb that means "to rebel," "to revolt," or "to transgress." It suggests a more willful decision to defy God's teaching and choose to go one's own way.

The psalmist does not claim to deserve forgiveness: His plea is based on Yahweh's constancy of mercy and steadfast love, which "have been from of old" (v. 6). This is covenant language, a clear echo of God's self-description to Moses: "The LORD, the LORD, a God merciful and gracious, slow to anger, and abounding in steadfast love and faithfulness, keeping steadfast love for the thousandth generation, forgiving iniquity and transgression and sin" (Exod. 34:6-7).

Thus, the psalmist appeals to God's faithfulness rather than his own worthiness: to bless him with grace rather than with what he deserves. ⚜

The poet's request that Yahweh would not remember his youthful sins, but would "remember" him according to the divine nature of steadfast love and goodness involves more than just hoping God will keep him in mind. In texts such as this, "to remember" is an internal act that has external consequences: God might remember someone because punishment is in order, or remember the obedient by bestowing blessings. The psalmist knows he has not earned God's favor; thus he appeals to God's mercy, love, and goodness.

⚜ **Emphatic pronouns:** The psalmist stresses the earnestness of his plea for forgiveness in v. 7b, though English versions rarely make any attempt to capture it. Hebrew does not require pronouns to be spelled out in many cases, including this one, but when the poet says "according to your steadfast love, remember me, for your goodness' sake, O LORD" (NRSV), a more literal translation would be "according to your steadfast love, remember me—you—for the sake of your goodness, O Yahweh." The noted Hebrew linguist Robert Alter translates it as "In Your kindness, recall me—You; for the sake of your goodness, O LORD."[2]

John I Durham has written of the psalmist: "He can count on Yahweh's consistency to provide what he needs rather than what he deserves, and thus prays to be remembered in accord with Yahweh's unchanging love and goodness."[3]

For reflection: *If God were to "remember you" as described above, would it be good news or bad news?*

BELIEVE ME . . .
(vv. 8-10)

The psalmist turns from prayer to testimony in vv. 8-10, no longer addressing God but whoever might read his poem or hear it recited in worship. Believing that God has heard his prayer, he declares to all that Yahweh is indeed "good and upright," a God who willingly "instructs sinners in the way," as he has asked (vv. 4-5).

Such guidance is offered to those who respectfully seek it, for "He leads the humble in what is right, and teaches the humble his way" (v. 9). This reflects the poet's own reverential approach as expressed in the previous verses.

The psalmist does not envision a revolving-door relationship of repetitive sin and forgiveness, as if our wrongdoing doesn't matter so long as we can call upon God's mercy. While he insists that "All the paths of the LORD are steadfast love and faithfulness," he also holds that such love and faithfulness are intended "for those who keep his covenant and his decrees" (v. 10). The more the psalmist learns about God's ways, the more he trusts, and the more faithful he becomes.

As the psalmist has come to believe these things about his relationship with God, he wants others to believe that they can also turn from their transgressions and experience undeserved but wondrous grace.

Some lessons are timeless. This is one of them. ♦

⚑**In short:** John I Durham summarizes the psalm's message this way: "It was the conviction of the poet of Psalm 25 that trust placed in God is well placed, and his desire was thus a fuller knowledge of God's ways so that he might trust more and more by following in them. His prayer is for protection, guidance, forgiveness, and deliverance. And his lesson is one of faith and consequent action. Both the prayer and the lesson remain much needed."[4]

THE HARDEST QUESTION
How do we want God to remember us?

The Hebrew verb translated as "remember" (*zākar*), used once in v. 6 and twice in v. 7, could be used in three primary ways:[5]

1. for wholly mental acts of calling to mind or paying attention to something or someone
2. an inner act of recollection that leads to a corresponding external act
3. to refer to someone speaking in the sense of "to recite" or "to invoke."

The second option is common: Gen. 8:1 declares that God brought the flood to an end because "God *remembered* Noah and all the wild animals and all the domestic animals that were with him in the ark. And God made a wind blow over the earth, and the waters subsided." God was later motivated to deliver Israel from Egypt, according to Exod. 2:24, because "God heard their groaning, and God *remembered* his covenant with Abraham, Isaac, and Jacob." King Hezekiah experienced healing after he prayed for God to *remember* his past faithfulness (2 Kgs. 20:3).

But remembering could also result in negative actions. Hos. 8:1 speaks of God's desire to bring healing to Israel: "But they do not consider that I *remember* all their wickedness. Now their deeds surround them, they are before my face." The author of Psalm 79, writing in behalf of all Israel rather than the individual context of Psalm 25, prayed that God would forget the sins of the ancestors and the punishment they deserved:

Do not *remember* against us the iniquities of our ancestors;
    let your compassion come speedily to meet us,
    for we are brought very low.
Help us, O God of our salvation,
    for the glory of your name;
    deliver us, and forgive our sins,
    for your name's sake. (Ps. 79:8-9)

The writer of Psalm 79, like the author of Psalm 25, knew that the forgiveness that comes with forgetting past sins is undeserved. Thus, he prays for the "God of our salvation" to "*not remember*" the nation's iniquities, but to act "for the glory of your name," bringing deliverance and forgiveness "for your name's sake."

In Psalm 25, the writer's request also falls mainly into the second category in the list above: He prays that God will not remember the sins of his youth (which could lead to well-deserved punishment), while boldly imploring Yahweh (with an imperative form of the verb) to remember him—that is, to act toward him—on the basis of grace and mercy that grows from God's steadfast love. Thus, it is no accident that the psalmist precedes his request that God *not remember* his youthful sins but *remember* him for the sake of God's inherent goodness by asking Yahweh to *call to mind* (or *remember*, the verb is the same) God's own mercy and steadfast love that "have been from of old" (v. 6).

Do we want God to remember us? Many of us may prefer that God forget about us altogether, lest we suffer from what our failures deserve, but that would be self-defeating. Like the psalmist, we want God to remember us, but selectively—forgetting our past sins and looking at us in the light of God's own mercy and faithful love.

Understanding the background of this Hebrew word may also be helpful as we think of those who have caused us pain. Are we willing to "not remember" past wrongs in order to live with generous grace toward others in the present?

Jesus reminded his followers that if they expected God to forget/forgive their sins, they would need to act in the same way toward others: "For if you forgive others their trespasses, your heavenly Father will also forgive you; but if you do not forgive others, neither will your Father forgive your trespasses" (Matt. 6:14-15).

When we consider our lives, on what basis dare we ask God to remember us?

NOTES

[1]Peter C. Craigie, *Psalms 1-50*, Word Bible Commentary (Waco: Word Books: 1983), 217-19.

[2]Robert Alter, *The Book of Psalms: A Translation with Commentary* (New York: W.W. Norton & Co., 2007), 85.

[3]John I Durham, "Psalms," in *The Broadman Bible Commentary*, vol. 4 (Nashville: Broadman Press, 1971), 221.

[4]Ibid., 222.

[5]Andrew Boling, "zākar," *Theological Wordbook of the Old Testament* (Chicago: Moody Bible Institute, 1980), entry 551.

Psalm 78:1-8

WE'RE IN TROUBLE NOW

We will not hide them from their children;
we will tell to the coming generation the glorious deeds of the LORD, and his might,
and the wonders that he has done.
—Psalm 78:4

If asked to name their favorite book in the Old Testament, it's likely that more people would choose the book of Psalms than any other. The psalms reflect the reality of our lives through pain and praise, rage and rejoicing, pride and penitence. It's no wonder that we turn to them again and again.

We should not forget that the psalms served as Israel's hymnbook. Their words are couched in lyrical fashion, and occasional introductory notes offer enigmatic hints as to how the song was to be performed. If only we knew the tunes!

You may find it helpful to read the words and then imagine what musical style the writer would have adopted if he or she were writing a similar song today. When I read Psalm 78, I find an unmistakable quality that sounds like the blues.

GOD SINGS THE BLUES

We can't do justice to vv. 1-8 without some appreciation for the entire psalm, but neither can we give appropriate attention to all 72 verses, so we'll settle for an overview. Scholars have attached a variety of labels to Psalm 78. It clearly begins with a theme common to Israel's wisdom teachers, but the latter part has been called everything from a descriptive hymn of praise to a meditation or philosophy of history. Throughout, there is a strong sense of lamentation over Israel's failures.

A close look shows that the text also has strong theological and political overtones—and in ancient Israel the two were rarely separate. While civil societies rightly maintain a separation of church and state, Israel's identity as a nation was inseparable from the people's covenant with God.

⬆ **The psalm's bones:**
Psalm 78 moves back and
forth through Israel's history
in attempting to teach an
important lesson for Israel's
future. The psalm is lengthy,
and moves constantly between
themes of God's provision,
judgment, and grace on the
one hand, and Israel's stubborn
rebellion and forgetfulness on
the other hand.

The psalm defies a neat
or simple outline. The following outline, suggested by
R. J. Clifford, sees the structure
as an introduction followed
by two "recitals" that follow
roughly the same order:[1]

Introduction (vv. 1-11)

First Recital:
Wilderness events (vv. 12-32)
Gracious act (vv. 12-16)
Rebellion (vv. 17-20)
Divine anger and punishment
   (vv. 21-32)
Sequel (vv. 33-39)

Second Recital:
From Egypt to Cannan
   (vv. 40-64)
Gracious act (vv. 40-55)
Rebellion (vv. 56-58)
Divine anger and punishment
   (vv. 59-64)
Sequel (vv. 65-72)

The primary purpose of Psalm 78 is to challenge hearers to learn a positive lesson from the negative example of Israel's history. It does this through a succession of reminders recounting God's deliverance and provision. It laments Israel's stubborn and persistent rebellion while recalling how God had responded with both judgment and grace. As a second-ary function, the psalm concludes with an affirmation of the Davidic dynasty as God's choice to rule over the Hebrews. ⬆

Some scholars have suggested that the psalm may have been written as early as the 10th century BCE, while others date it as late as the post-exilic period. Though it does not specifically mention the division of the kingdoms following Solomon's death around 930 BCE or the destruction of the Northern Kingdom (referred to in the psalm as "Israel" or "Ephraim") in 722 BCE, the psalm seems to presume it.

One who reads through the entire psalm cannot help but share the psalmist's frustra-tion over Israel's historical pattern of divine deliverance followed by human rebellion. God gave the people of Israel covenant rules to live by, worked miracles on their behalf, delivered them from Egypt, provided food and water in the wilderness, showed grace and patience beyond measure—and was perpetu-ally thanked with forgetfulness, complaints, sinfulness, and rebellion. Note, for example, that vv. 19b-20 reflect a virtual denial of Psalm 23's reference to God preparing a table, as the people ask "Can God spread a table in the wilderness? Even though he struck the rock so that water gushed out and torrents overflowed, can he also give bread or provide meat for his people?"

ꙮ **Psalming the blues:** Here's my attempt to recast Psalm 78 as a traditional blues song, sung by the narrator of the psalm:[2]

Well the Lord looked down on Israel, didn't like what he saw—
They were living as slaves in Egypt making bricks without any straw—
So he sent Moses to his people, and plagues upon Pharaoh,
He led them through the Red Sea, and on dry land they did go,
He brought them out of Egypt, and he set his people free,
But soon they turned their backs on him and chose idolatry,
    They give me the blues—I got the Israelite blues—
      I got the idolizin' compromisin' ugly livin' Israelite blues . . .

They were traveling through the desert, and they had no food to eat,
No water they could drink or even cool their blistered feet,
So the Lord sent bread from heaven, and quail upon the wind,
And water from a rock so that they all could drink it in,
But the more the Lord had blessed them, the more they all complained,
They said they wanted caviar and rocks filled with champagne,
    They give me the blues—I got the Israelite blues—
      I got the fussin' cussin' sinnin' grinnin' wicked men and willful women blues . . .

The Lord brought them 'cross the Jordan, into the promised land.
He delivered every enemy into the army's hand,
But they soon forgot the One who had given victory,
They acted like the Canaanites and worshiped every tree,
They gave their hearts to Baal and their gifts to Asherah,
They failed to teach their children how to pray and love the law,
    They give me the blues—I got the Israelite blues—
      I got the idolizin' compromisin' ugly livin' Israelite blues . . .

Well the Lord gave up on Ephraim, but in Judah he did trust,
He gave the throne to David and said make it there or bust,
So now we have a kingdom, and our king is David's son,
We hope that he will lead us to be faithful to the One,
Who brought us out from Egypt and who blessed us on the way,
We hope that we'll remember and we hope we will not stray,
    But we get the blues—we get the Israelite blues—
      We get the fussin' cussin' sinnin' grinnin' wicked men and willful women blues.

In keeping with the covenant rules set out in the law, God was compelled to judge the people when they turned to other gods, though always careful to temper judgment with grace and hope that the people would yet learn their lesson and become faithful.

The song is, without question, a royal downer. Despite God's best efforts, nothing had gone right and the only hope that remained was that David's descendants might do better. It is this constant theme of human stubbornness and failure that makes the psalm so blue: the poet was inspired to imagine how God was singing the blues over Israel. ♦

RIDDLE ME THIS
(vv. 1-4)

> ♦ **The making of a *maskil*:** The superscription to Psalm 78 labels it a "*maskil*." The term is derived from a Hebrew verb that means "to be prudent," or "to ponder." That is a fitting description of this psalm, which is designed to inspire meditation on how one should act in response to God's goodness, especially in the light of Israel's history. We would also do well to ponder its message.

Psalm 78 begins in the fashion of typical wisdom teachings, with an imperative call for people to heed the speaker and learn from his words (v. 1). These words are in the form of a "parable" or "dark sayings from of old" (v. 2). ♦

The word translated as "parable" is the same word (*mashal*) typically used for proverbial statements that are usually much shorter than Psalm 78. The book of Proverbs, for example, is a collection of *meshalim*, the plural form of *mashal*. Both short proverbs and this lengthy psalm are told with an intent to teach.

The poet's parable, however, is a paradox. The word behind "dark sayings" commonly means "riddle." Wisdom teachers of the ancient Near East often used riddles as teaching methods, and the Hebrews were no different. In this case, the writer doesn't claim to ask a question with a trick answer. The riddle he tells is an unsolved question, a puzzle for pondering: How is it that Israel could persistently respond to God's grace and goodness with rebellion rather than repentance, with sin instead of obedience?

The call to learn from the past for the sake of the present and the hope of the future is a common theme in the Old Testament. The psalmist emphasizes the deep roots of the story he is about to tell, the history he is about to recount, in a variety of ways. His riddles are "of old," (v. 2), he says, as he relates "things . . . that our ancestors have told us" (v. 3).

The psalmist declares his determination to keep the traditions alive, even when they are painful. The people should not hide past failures from future generations, any more than they should hide God's "glorious deeds" in Israel's behalf (v. 4). The poet may have had in mind Moses' call for the Israelites to love God with all their heart, soul, and strength; to remember God's commandments; and to conscientiously pass them on to their children from generation to generation (Deut. 6:4-9). ⬇

⬇ **Hear, and teach:** The famous words found in Deut. 6:4-9 are called the "Shema" (sh-MAH), after the first word in Hebrew, the imperative "Hear!" Faithful Jews continue to recite this text and place tiny scrolls containing it inside ornamental mezzusahs, which they attach to their doorposts. Orthodox Jews follow v. 9 literally by placing certain scriptures inside small leather boxes (called phylacteries) and binding them to their upper arm and forehead when they pray.

Here's the text, from the NRSV: "Hear, O Israel: The LORD our God, the LORD is one. Love the LORD your God with all your heart and with all your soul and with all your strength. These commandments that I give you today are to be upon your hearts. Impress them on your children. Talk about them when you sit at home and when you walk along the road, when you lie down and when you get up. Tie them as symbols on your hands and bind them on your foreheads. Write them on the doorframes of your houses and on your gates" (Deut. 6:4-9).

For reflection: *To what extent are your current faith and your relation to the church influenced by what your parents passed on to you?*

HERE'S THE DEAL
(vv. 5-8)

The psalmist could not charge Israel with failure without a reminder of the rules the people had violated, so the teacher reminds readers (or hearers) how Israel had willingly entered a covenant with God. Note the poetic inclusion of both the southern tribes (indicated by "Jacob") and the northern tribes (indicated by "Israel") in v. 5: "He established a decree in Jacob, and appointed a law in Israel."

The verse consists of two couplets, and in each of them the second line amplifies the meaning of the first. The word for "decree" can also mean "testimony" or "law," and in v. 5 its sense is clarified by the use of the parallel term *torah*, or "law," in the second line of the couplet.

It was not enough to give the law to the Exodus generation alone, however. The covenant was to be binding on all future generations. Thus, for the people to remain faithful to their special relationship with God, they must not only live by it, but also pass it on to their children, who would teach it to the next generation, not yet born (v. 6).

The psalmist understood that Israel was always just one generation from forgetting their special covenant with God: If the current generation did not both practice and preach the law that bound them in relationship with Yahweh, there would be little hope for Israel's future.

If the people faithfully passed on their faith, however, future Hebrews would understand that they are to "set their hope in God, and not forget the works of God, but keep his commandments" (v. 7). This would be the ideal scenario: parents committed to passing on their faith and practice from generation to generation.

The psalmist's introductory thoughts continue through v. 8, where we learn the sad truth that many in Israel had not lived up to their calling. They had not remembered their responsibilities to God, but chose to follow other paths and worship other gods. Thus, the writer speaks of ancestors he describes as "a stubborn and rebellious generation, a generation whose heart was not steadfast, whose spirit was not faithful to God" (v. 8).

The psalmist apparently has in mind the very first generation to be called Israel, the very people who had been delivered from Egypt and who solemnly entered a binding covenant with God at Sinai. The remainder of the psalm recounts in graphic detail the many ways in which that generation ignored or forgot God's many displays of grace and provision, choosing to complain about what they didn't have rather than appreciating what God had provided.

The teacher who composed Psalm 78 was convinced that Israel's people were poor students of history, failing to learn from the past—and that left God singing the blues.

For reflection: *As Christian believers read this text, Israel's wilderness wandering may seem far distant and not applicable to our lives. While we do not relate to God based on the same covenant under which Israel lived, we do live in a relationship with God based on the grace God has shown through Christ and our response to God's redemptive acts. Every generation of believers is responsible for passing on its faith. What are some concrete ways in which we may help children and others to understand our past for the sake of the present and the hope of the future?*

THE HARDEST QUESTION
Does God kill without cause?

The hardest question relative to Psalm 78 does not come from the introductory section, but from deeper in the psalm. Those who read through the entire psalm may be taken aback by vv. 30-31, which claim that God killed the best of the Israelites for no apparent cause. When the people had complained about having only manna to eat, the text says, God sent flocks of quail, more than the people could eat:

But before they had satisfied their craving,
    while the food was still in their mouths,
the anger of God rose against them
    and he killed the strongest of them,
    and laid low the flower of Israel.

How are we to understand this troublesome text? First, we note that in vv. 21-31 the psalmist is recounting the tradition found in Num. 11:1-35, with some embellishment. The Numbers account of a "great plague" is expanded with the statement that God intentionally selected the choicest Israelites to kill. Did God kill without cause?

If we return to Numbers 11, we find a similar account in vv. 1-3: When the people complained excessively, God became angry and "the fire of the LORD burned against them, and consumed some of the outlying parts of the camp" (v. 1b). When the people asked Moses to intercede, he prayed for them "and the fire abated" (v. 2b).

The next verse begins with a reference to certain "rabble among them" who "had a strong craving" and instigated a public cry for meat, recalling the finer fare they had enjoyed in Egypt. This raised God's ire, and is paralleled in Ps. 78:21-22, which says God was "full of rage; a fire was kindled against Jacob, his anger mounted against Israel, because they had no faith in God, and did not trust his saving power."

In both Numbers and Psalms, then, God was portrayed as already being angry at the people's faithlessness prior to sending enough manna and quail to stuff their gullets to bursting.

The judgment, in the form of a plague (according to Num. 11:33) that struck the strongest Israelites (according to Ps. 78:31), is thus to be understood as being in response to the earlier complaints, timed to coincide with the fulfillment of the people's demand for meat.

The collusion of deliverance and judgment seems harsh to modern ears, but made perfect sense to the teachers of Israel, who firmly believed that blessing or cursing followed tit for tat upon obedience or rebellion. Arthur Weiser observed that the account demonstrates "how closely God's grace and his judgment are related to each other."[3]

Modern readers may still quail at the thought of God unleashing divine anger on the weak and complaining Israelites, but the teacher behind Psalm 78 was convinced that God had good cause to do so.

NOTES

[1]R. J. Clifford, from "In Zion and David a New Beginning: An Interpretation of Psalm 78," in *Traditions in Transformation*, ed. Frank Moore Cross (Winona Lake: Eisenbraun's, 1981), 121-41; cited by Marvin E. Tate in *Psalms 51-100*, Word Biblical Commentary (Waco: Word Books, 1990), 287.

[2]A video version of the song can be found at: http://www.nurturingfaith.net/adult-archives/category/november-2011.

[3]Arthur Weiser, *The Psalms: A Commentary*, trans. H. Hartwell, Old Testament Library (Philadelphia: Westminster Press, 1962), 541.

Psalm 80

GET ME OUT OF HERE!

Restore us, O God;
let your face shine, that we may be saved.
—Psalm 80:3

D o you sometimes think your prayers go unanswered because God is angry with you? Do you ever get angry with God because you cry out and it seems that God remains silent? Have you made promises, on occasion, that if God would just answer your prayer, you'd do certain things in return?

If so, you're not the first. Those themes are common in Israel's hymnbook, which contained many laments, including Psalm 80. We can't be sure how the psalm came about, ♥ but what's important is that it emerged from a perspective of deep loss and frustration. The psalmist wrote in behalf of a people who had lost their pride, their power, and their position as a world leader.

If the people of Israel had owned hound dogs and pick-up trucks, no doubt they would have lost them, too. That's why I'm convinced that if this psalmist had written his song today, it would have been a country song. ♥

♥ **What was the trouble?:**
Scholars have put forward many ideas about the situation in history that led to this plaintive psalm. Some suggest it was written in the northern kingdom of Israel, around 722 BCE, when the Assyrians were ravaging the land. The "Joseph" tribes of Ephraim and Manasseh are mentioned, along with Benjamin—and they were all northern tribes. In support of this view, the Septuagint adds "concerning the Assyrians" to the superscription.

Even so, others think the psalm may have come from a troublesome time in the southern kingdom, from the years in exile, or even from the early post-exilic period. Though the author in those settings would have been from Judah, references to tribes from the defunct northern kingdom could have expressed a wish for the remaining Hebrews to be reunited.

♆ **A sad country song:** Like most country songs, Psalm 80 has a chorus that's repeated several times. You'll find the chorus in verses 3, 7, and 19: "Restore us O God; let your face shine, that we may be saved." The first verse of the song is vv. 1-2 of the text. The second verse is vv. 4-6. The third verse is longer: vv. 8-18. Imagine what it might sound like in more contemporary language, with an old-style country beat.[1]

Chorus (vv. 3, 7, 19)
Bring back the light, show us your face,
Break through our night, so we'll all be saved,
Oh shine your love into this dark place,
Bring back the light of your amazing grace.

Verse 1 (vv. 1-2)
Give ear O shepherd of Israel,
Look down from heaven, you know us well.
Stir up your power and save us, please—
we come before you on bended knees.

(Chorus)

Verse 2 (vv. 4-6)
You seem too angry to hear our prayers,
You feed us bread that's soaked with tears.
Our neighbors scorn us, our enemies smirk,
You've run us down with your judgment truck.

(Chorus)

Verses 3 & 4 (vv. 8-13, 14-18)
You made us like a growing vine,
Planted us down deep on a mountainside.
We spread like kudzu, clear to the sea,
But now we're pig food, won't you hear our plea?

Look down upon us and see this vine,
We have been bush-hogged and burned with fire.
Restore our future, so hope remains,
Then we'll be faithful, and call your name.

(Chorus, sing last line twice)

One of the central themes of country music is the element of loss . . . lost love, lost happiness, lost opportunities. This song speaks of many deprivations, but the most heartfelt loss is the presence of God.

RESTORE US, O GOD . . .
(vv. 1-3)

Psalm 80 is preceded by a lengthy superscription that probably has to do with the song's tune. ♻ The psalm is a prime example of a communal lament in which a leader either sang in behalf of the larger group, or led them all in singing a plaintive prayer to God. Laments typically contain an address to God, a complaint about the worshiper(s)' present plight, and a plea for help. Promises to praise God in return for answered prayer are also common.

A threefold appeal for Yahweh to save (vv. 3, 7, 19) divides the psalm into three unequal parts: an invocation and appeal (vv. 1-3), a complaint (vv. 4-7), and an extended metaphor comparing Israel to a vine, concluding with a vow (vv. 8-19). ♻ ♻ ♻

♻ **Name that tune:** Psalm 80's complex superscription appears to instruct the leader to use a tune that includes the word "Lilies," though some scholars have speculated that the term *shoshannim* could also refer to an otherwise unknown stringed instrument.

The psalm is also identified as an *"eduth,"* and belonging to a collection attributed to Asaph. *Eduth* can be translated as "covenant" (NRSV) or "testimony" (HCSB), but many interpreters believe it should be read in conjunction with *shoshannin.* Thus, the NIV has "According to [the tune of] 'The Lilies of the Covenant.'" The uncertainty of translation leads some versions to simply transliterate the Hebrew words either singly (NAS95) or in combination (KJV, NET).

♻ **Say again:** The thrice-repeated chorus (vv. 3, 7, 19) is identical except for the divine names used in the address. Verse 3 addresses "God" (*elohim*), v. 7 appeals to "God of Hosts" (*elohim sabaôt*), and v. 19 calls out to "Yahweh God of Hosts" (usually translated LORD God of Hosts," *Yahweh elohim sabaôt*). In deference to English style, most translations begin the address with the exclamation "O," but there is no equivalent in the Hebrew.

Scholars have suggested many explanations for the differing titles. The most appealing to me is that the poet or a later editor sought to add emphasis to each repetition of the chorus by using progressively more complex variations in appealing to God.

⬥ **All together now:** "Restore us" translates the hiphil stem of the verb *shub*, which means "to turn," "to return," or by extension, "to repent." While the psalmist may simply be asking God to return Israel to an earlier situation of peace and security, the prayer has overtones of asking God to "turn us around" or "cause us to repent," which the poet believed would lead to the same result: that "we shall be saved."

⬥ **"If you . . . then I . . .":** Hebrew vows, unlike the modern concept of vow making, were not like wedding vows or monastic vows, which are designed to be unconditional pledges. Rather, they are clear conditional promises that ask God for something and promise something in return.[3]

Hannah, for example, asked God for a son, and promised to return him to God's service (1 Sam. 1:11).

The people of Israel promised that if God gave them victory over the Canaanite king of Arad, they would devote all of the plunder to God (Num. 21:1-3).

Vows may also be found in the psalms, as in vv. 17-18 of Psalm 80:

But let your hand be upon the one at your right hand,
    the one whom you made strong for yourself.
Then we will never turn back from you;
    give us life, and we will call on your name.

The initial appeal for God to hear—cast boldly as an imperative verb—employs three participle phrases as divine epithets. "Shepherd of Israel," "you who lead Joseph like a flock," and "you who sit enthroned between the cherubim" (v. 1) all recall earlier periods when God was thought to have led Israel in visible ways, as during the exodus from Egypt. ⬥

The community pleads for the exalted God who has led them in the past to "shine forth" before Ephraim, Benjamin, and Manasseh—to "awaken" in power; and to come with salvation. But why mention only three tribes, when tradition names twelve?

Note that the psalm invokes God's attention with images from Israel's memory of how God—enthroned above the Ark of the Covenant—led Israel in the wilderness. Num. 2:17-24 says that when the Israelites set out on each stage of their wilderness journey, the first three tribes to follow the Ark were Ephraim, Benjamin, and Manasseh: the same order as Ps. 80:2. It is as if the psalmist is praying for God to come again and lead the tribes through their present trial.

⏺ **Follow the leader:** Verse 1 mentions Joseph, while v. 2 names Ephraim, Benjamin, and Manasseh. Joseph was remembered as the full brother of Benjamin (their parents were Jacob and Rachel), and the father of Ephraim and Manasseh, who became the largest of the tribes. When Jacob blessed his grandsons Ephraim and Manasseh, he claimed that God had been his shepherd for his entire life (Gen. 48:15).

The familiar notion of God as a guiding shepherd was also present in the Exodus account (Exod. 15:13), in the prophets (Ezek. 34:11-16, 31), and in other psalms (Ps. 23, 100:3).

The image of God as being enthroned between or above the cherubim is drawn from the description of the sacred Ark of the Covenant, topped by two golden cherubim, as a locus for God's special presence (Exod. 25:19-22, Num. 7:89, 1 Sam. 4:4, 2 Sam. 6:2).

In the Lxodus narratives, the Ark of the Covenant was carried at the head of the procession as the Israelites traveled from Sinai to the land of promise, following God's symbolic presence in a cloud by day and a pillar of fire by night (Exod. 13:21-22, Num. 14:14, Neh. 9:12). And, according to Num. 2:17-24, the first three tribes in line were Ephraim, Benjamin, and Manasseh.

The images of God's awakening to Israel's plight, shining forth, and coming to save are echoed in the first instance of the repeated refrain: "Restore us, O God; make your face shine upon us, that we may be saved" (v. 3, see also vv. 7 and 20).

God's face was traditionally thought to shine with glory, so much that Moses' face also shone after being in God's presence (Exod. 34:29). But the expression may also reflect a cultural background in which gods do battle with each other, with the winners "shining forth" in victory. Examples can be found in Canaanite literature.[2] Similar images of the "divine shine" are found in Ps. 50:2 and 94:1.

Readers may also contemplate a connection with the Aaronic blessing of Num. 6:24-26: "The LORD bless you and keep you; the LORD make his face to shine upon you, and be gracious to you; the LORD lift up his countenance upon you, and give you peace."

Calling upon God to "shine forth" was a poetic way of asking God to show favor toward Israel and come with saving power.

For reflection: *The psalmist used an imperative verb in addressing God, in essence beginning his prayer with "Listen to me, O shepherd of Israel!" Do you dare to pray with such boldness? Do you think it's appropriate?*

LET YOUR FACE SHINE UPON US …
(vv. 4-7)

Why would this request be appropriate? Because the people seem convinced that God is furious with them and no longer listens to their prayers. God's face, rather than shining forth in favor, is wreathed in smoke from God's smoldering anger (v. 4).

The people have been praying, the psalmist implies, but God has responded with fumes rather than favor. The question is how long (literally, "until when?") this state of affairs will continue.

Indeed, the psalm laments that God actively opposes the people: While they have prayed for merciful deliverance, God has given them "the bread of tears" to eat and buckets of tears to drink (v. 5). ⬮

And why so many tears? "You have made us a source of contention to our neighbors," the psalmist cried, "and our enemies mock us" (v. 6). Note the direct accusation that God is the source of the people's trouble. This is not out of line with the traditional Old Testament belief that God's favor mirrors human behavior.

> ⬮ **Torrents of tears:** The term "bowlful" (NRSV) as a measure of tears to be drunk translates the word *shalish*, which means "a third." Here it refers to a third of a larger measure, just as we think of a "quart" as a fourth of a gallon. Unfortunately, the text doesn't say which larger measure the psalmist has in mind, but the clear implication is that Israel drank tears in quantity. Whether we think of kegs, steins, jugs, or buckets, the image is clear.

This theology, especially clear in the book of Deuteronomy (classically expressed in ch. 28), lies behind the contention of the books of Judges, Samuel, and Kings that God used foreign nations as divine agents to punish the Hebrews when they chose to reject God's leadership and follow other gods.

The books of Job and Ecclesiastes thoroughly questioned the adequacy of such a quid pro quo theology, and the New Testament ushered in a new covenant in which salvation comes by grace rather than works. Even so, the notion that "you get what you deserve" remains a popular belief.

In the psalmist's mind, good or bad fortune was always divinely determined. We may not hold to the same theology, but we still have a tendency to blame our troubles on God rather than accepting responsibility for our own actions. As a result, we sometimes think of God more as a cosmic repairman we call on to fix things rather than a loving shepherd we follow every day.

For reflection: *If we give God credit for the blessings we enjoy, should we also blame God when tragedy or hard times come? Why do you think as you do?*

THAT WE MAY BE SAVED
(vv. 8-19)

In vv. 8-16, the psalmist employs an extended metaphor, portraying God as an active horticulturalist who took a grape vine (Israel) from Egypt, cleared out the promised land like a fertile field, and transplanted the vine in a new home (vv. 8-9). The verdant vine then spread from the mountains of the southern Negev to the cedars of Lebanon, from the Mediterranean Sea to the Euphrates River—borders that were promised in Deut. 11:22-25 and may have been realized approximately under David and Solomon's rule (vv. 10-11).

But that was in the past. The psalm declares that God had broken down the protective walls of the vineyard, allowing anyone to pick its fruit and wild animals to ravage it (vv. 12-13, compare Isa. 5:1-7). The community cries out as the personified vine, pleading for God to have pity on it as "the son you have raised up for yourself" (v. 15), but which has been cut and burned (v. 16).

The request of favor for "the man at your right hand" parallels "the son of man you have raised up for yourself" (vv. 15, 17). While some commentators speculate that this is a reference to Benjamin (whose name means "son of the right hand") or to a particular king, the more straightforward allusion is to Israel, the vine that God had initially blessed and later cursed.

How could the community attract God's attention, change God's mind, and persuade God to shine forth with renewed favor and deliverance?

In times of extremity, ancient peoples often resorted to making vows to God, conditional promises that ask God for something, and promise something in return.

Thus, the prayer for the hand of God's blessing in v. 17 is followed by the promise "then we will not turn away from you" (v. 18a). The vow is then repeated, in different words: "Revive us, and (then) we will call on your name" (v. 18b).

The closing verse repeats the refrain found in vv. 3 and 7, asking God to come with shining face to deliver the people from their trouble. Playing "Let's Make a Deal" with God is nothing new.

For reflection: *Does this psalm reflect the way we pray? When we find ourselves in distress, are we likely to try swinging a deal with God? Have we ever prayed like this: "Oh God, if you will get me out of this mess, I promise to straighten up"—or "I promise to get back in church," or "I'll do whatever you want me to do"? Is there a better way to pray?*

THE HARDEST QUESTION
What's wrong—or right—with this prayer?

Psalm 80 is clearly a part of scripture, and it is a prayer. Does that mean it provides an appropriate pattern for prayer? Keep in mind that it reflects Israel's approach to God in a particular setting, and Israel did not always get it right. We can learn from both negative and positive examples.

What's wrong with the prayer? First, the prayer appears to approach God as one whose primary business is bailing us out. We all are created in the image of God, who gives us both the right and the responsibility to make personal decisions for good or evil. There are times when trouble comes calling with no invitation, but often the trouble we experience is of our own making.

I have known people who didn't learn to take responsibility because their parents were always coming behind them and cleaning up their messes and taking up for them even when they were clearly at fault. When that happens, we have difficulty learning to accept responsibility for our own actions. It's all too easy to blame someone else and expect others to bail us out of trouble.

The Old Testament narratives repeatedly recount (read the book of Judges!) how the people of Israel were prone to rebellion against God, falling into idolatry, living immoral lives, and generally turning their backs on the way God had taught them to live. When they got in trouble, however, they had a tendency to start acting religious. There was something wrong with that then, and there's something wrong with that now.

A second thing wrong with the prayer is that it tries to swing a deal with God. The prayer concludes with a promise that, if God will only save Israel, then they will be faithful and worship God as they should. Many of us have prayed that same sort of prayer. Because humans are prone to making deals, we assume that God is, too. But God loves us for who we are, not just for what we do. God wants to forgive us and cleanse us and help us start anew because we come in repentance desiring a better life—not because God needs or wants whatever payoff we might promise.

There is at least one thing right about this prayer: It acknowledges that in some matters, only God can help. When it comes to a redemptive and eternal relationship with God, only God can help us with that.

We may also face other times when trouble comes, whether self-inflicted or not, and we know that only God can help, and it is appropriate to seek God's aid. It is important, however, to understand that there are no guarantees. God promises to love us and care for us and be present with us. God does not, however, promise to make life easy for us, or to always say "yes" when we ask for something.

It is true that sometimes, when we pray, it seems that God is silent. God may seem silent because we don't know how to listen, or don't take the time. God may seem silent because the answer to our prayer is not "yes," and that's the only answer we are listening for. Sometimes, however, the heavens seem quiet because God *is* silent (compare 1 Kgs. 19:11-12). Sometimes silence is the most powerful way of speaking. Sometimes God's apparent absence may be what it takes to make us hungrier for God's presence.

And sometimes, the answer we need is "no." I suspect most of us can think of things we once asked for with all our hearts, but looking back, we realize that we are better off now because that prayer was not answered with a "yes."

There may be other areas that we don't understand and maybe in this life we never will, for example: why God didn't stop the cancer, why God didn't keep loved ones safe from all physical harm. Some things we won't understand until we get a chance to stand face to face and ask God ourselves. When that time comes, some of us may have quite a list. In the meantime, though, we live by trust and faith that God does hear our prayer, and that God's presence is sure even when divine intervention is not.

NOTES

[1]You can hear what the song might sound like at http://www.nurturingfaith.net/adult-archives/category/november-2011.

[2]Marvin Tate, *Psalms 51-100*, Word Biblical Commentary (Waco: Word Books, 1990), 305.

[3]For more on vows in the psalms, see Tony Cartledge, "Conditional Vows In the Psalms of Lament: A New Approach to an Old Problem," in Ken Hoglund et al, eds., *The Listening Heart: Essays in Psalms and Wisdom in Honor of Roland E. Murphy, O. Carm.* (Sheffield, England: JSOT Press, 1987), 77-94.

Psalm 121

WILL AN EYE-LIFT HELP?

I lift up my eyes to the hills—
from where will my help come?
—Psalm 121:1

All of us need help now and then. Our difficulty may be something as simple as opening a stubborn jar of jelly, as complex as a blown head gasket, or as deep as an emotional crisis.

A stronger grip can handle the jar and a skilled mechanic can repair the car, but what do we do when the whole world seems dark or our heart is in shreds? To whom do we turn?

We don't know what troubles, fears, or insecurities the author of Psalm 121 faced, but he or she was also looking for help.

THE SOURCE OF HELP
(vv. 1-2)

Psalm 121 is called a "song of ascent," and may have been sung by pilgrims as they traveled to Jerusalem for one of the three annual festivals, or made the steep climb into the city itself. ♦

♦ **Going up?:** Psalm 121 is one of 15 psalms, collected together as Psalms 120-134, that begin with the superscription "A Song of Ascents." The precise meaning of this phrase is uncertain, but scholars commonly speculate that such songs arose for use by pilgrims as they journeyed to Jerusalem for one of the annual festivals, or on a personal pilgrimage to the temple.

Jerusalem is about 2,600 feet above sea level and thus not on a particularly high mountain, but it is surrounded by deep valleys, so from any direction, one has to "go up" or ascend in order to enter the city. As the site of the temple, the city was considered to be holy, so "going up" to Jerusalem carried a spiritual sense, too.

While this psalm came to be included in a collection of 15 psalms labeled as "songs of ascents" in Psalms 120-134, its origin could have been much earlier. The mention of David in the superscription might suggest that David wrote the psalm, but could just as easily mean that a psalm was dedicated to David.

Feeling a sense of need, the psalmist begins "I lift up my eyes to the hills: from where will my help come?" (v. 1). While a pilgrimage to one of the annual festivals might have provided an appropriate setting, the prayer could have been offered at any place, at any time.

The word for "hills" could also be translated as "mountains," but are these heights emblematic of inspiration or danger? Readers typically imagine the psalmist looking toward beautiful rolling hills or scenic mountains as a source of divine inspiration. Most mountains in Israel, however—especially those from Jerusalem and southward—are rugged and austere, fraught with danger for travelers.

Does the traveler feel fretful of the perils of his upcoming journey on a steep and hazardous road, or does she find in mountain majesty the assurance of divine aid for daily life?

Perhaps the distinction is not as important as the direction: the psalmist was *looking up*. Whether or not hills or mountains are in our line of sight, we often look heavenward, as the psalmist did, as we groan with sorrow or voice our prayer and wonder if there will be any help for us.

Looking up and offering a prayer implies a posture of hope, and posture alone can sometimes kick-start us on the path toward a better state of mind. This is especially true when we consciously look toward God, and that is precisely what the psalmist is doing, seeking help from "the LORD, who made heaven and earth." ♉

♉ **Creation and redemption:** By referring to "the LORD who created heaven and earth," the psalmist connects creation and redemption. Paul did this with respect to the life of Christ in Col. 1:15-20: "He is the image of the invisible God, the firstborn of all creation; for in him all things in heaven and on earth were created, things visible and invisible, whether thrones or dominions or rulers or powers—all things have been created through him and for him. He himself is before all things, and in him all things hold together. He is the head of the body, the church; he is the beginning, the firstborn from the dead, so that he might come to have first place in everything. For in him all the fullness of God was pleased to dwell, and through him God was pleased to reconcile to himself all things, whether on earth or in heaven, by making peace through the blood of his cross."

We might note that both the Apostles Creed and the Nicene Creed reflect v. 2, as they contain the affirmation "I believe in God the Father Almighty, maker of heaven and earth."

We know, of course, that God is not directional. God is every bit as much beneath our feet as above our heads, but we seem to be hard-wired to think of God as being up, or out. When we look up to God, we get the physical benefits of an uplifting posture and the spiritual benefits of putting our trust and our hopes in God. ☟

Surprisingly, churches filled with the most oppressed or downtrodden people tend to have the most joyful worship. Perhaps it is because they have learned that, no matter how heavy and how hard their burdens, standing together with heads up and hearts out, with hands and voices raised to heaven, brings a sense of comfort in believing one's prayer has been heard.

When we worship together, singing praise in the face of

☟ **Posture and positivity:** Social psychologist Amy Cuddy has done intriguing research on how our physical posture affects our mental outlook.[1] Cuddy discovered that an inward, drawn-in, head-down posture leads to a self-defeating attitude. By simply standing or sitting straight in an upward-looking "power pose" for just two minutes, the level of testosterone in our brains will go up, and the level of cortisol will go down.

For both men and women, an adequate level of testosterone boosts our feelings of confidence and makes us more assertive. On the other hand, cortisol is a stress hormone. The higher one's cortisol level, the more stressed one feels.

Improving our brain chemistry through a more confident posture won't answer our prayers, but it helps to put is in a receptive frame of mind.

troubles and trials, we feel less alone. We feel more hopeful. We feel stronger. We feel more confident that we can indeed make it another day, and another day, and another one after that. ☟

We believe there is a God, and that God is able to help.

For reflection: *Can you recall times when you have found strength by "looking up" to God through personal prayer or joining the community of fellow believers in worship?*

⚓ The power of hope: We learn from the psalmist that there is power in hope. That's one of the reasons God is so willing to hear our prayers, even when they're focused on complaints.

Of course, looking up, looking forward, looking to God does not mean that we forget where we are entirely. It doesn't mean that we ignore our own troubles and the troubled world around us and put our head in the clouds instead of the sand and just sing "In the sweet by and by" without giving attention to the bitter now and now. No, we work. We strive. We do our best to make things better both for ourselves and for others, but whether we succeed or not, we live on in hope.

More than 1500 years ago, in a commentary on Psalm 64—a psalm of deep lament in troubled times—Augustine echoed a similar thought, and challenged his readers to sing in the face of trouble and to look ahead with hope: "Now let us hear, brothers, let us hear and sing; let us pine for the city where we are citizens . . . By pining we are already there; we have already cast our hope like an anchor on that coast. I sing of somewhere else, not of here: for I sing with my heart, not with my flesh."[2]

THE SOURCE OF SECURITY
(vv. 3-6)

We say that we believe God is able to help, but how much practical help do we actually get? Can this psalm be believed?

On the surface, the text seems to promise that God will provide such perfect guidance and care that worshipers will suffer no harm or hardship in life, but we know from experience that this is manifestly not true. We all live in a world where bad things happen, and sometimes they happen to us.

Two observations can help us to appreciate the hopeful comfort of this psalm without either expecting too much of God or writing off the psalm as nothing more than wishful thinking.

The first thing is to note that the context of the psalm appears to be one of blessing or benediction. While the first two verses are written in the first person as the question and testimony of the worshiper, vv. 3-8 are written in the third person, as if someone else is responding to the question.

We might think of this psalm as a parting blessing shared by family or friends, but another likely scenario is to be found in worship, either at the beginning or the ending of a pilgrim festival. The congregation—or a representative worshiper—could chant or sing vv. 1-2, asking where one might find help while affirming that Yahweh is the creator of all things and thus the ultimate source of aid.

At that point a priest or chorus of temple singers might respond with vv. 3-8, offering words of blessing and benediction to those gathered. The verb forms in v. 3 can be read as either imperfect ("He will not let your foot be moved," NRSV) or jussive (a hopeful wish): "May he not allow your foot to slip" (NET).

If we translate the verbs in v. 3 as jussives, the psalm takes on the character of a blessing or benediction, even if the remaining verbs are rendered as promises.

It seems best to recognize that the psalm has characteristics of both blessing and promise, with the power of the blessing lying in the belief that God can indeed provide the help we seek.

"May he not let your foot slip" is not just a wish for sure footing on mountain paths, though it may include that, but is also an idiom for standing firm in life. Few people relish uncertainty, feeling lost or at loose ends.

Those who trust Yahweh have a "keeper" who never sleeps but constantly stands guard (v. 4). As a result, those who trust in Yahweh are never alone or unnoticed.

Take note of how often forms of the word "keep" appear in the psalm: vv. 3, 4, and 5 contain participles referring to "the one who keeps," while vv. 7 and 8 contain three uses of the imperfect form of the verb: "The LORD will keep."

The word translated "keep" (*shāmar*) is the same word used to describe a shepherd's keeping of the sheep. It suggests watching over, guiding, protecting, and being present with the flock.

Thus, "the LORD is your keeper" suggests a picture of one who keeps watch over the personified sheep of Israel or others who trust in Yahweh, one who stands ready at the right hand, where a favored counselor might be positioned.

Yahweh's protection extends to shelter from both sun and moon. The dangers of too much sun are obvious: The ancients would not have understood the relationship between ultraviolet light and skin cancer, but they would have been familiar with the uncomfortable heat, drying effects, and blistering of skin that come with too much sun.

But what of the moon? Modern people think nothing of walking beneath a full moon and may delight in it (unless they're afraid of vampires), but many ancient peoples believed that too much exposure to moonlight could lead to disease or even madness (the term "moonstruck" originally had nothing to do with love).

The presence of Yahweh, according to the psalmist, would provide protection from the moon's sinister rays, comforting pilgrims who might be camping out without a tent.

For reflection: *When you were a child, were you afraid of the dark? Were you taught any sort of bedtime prayer designed to comfort you with the promise of God's presence?*

THE SOURCE OF LIFE
(vv. 7-8)

With vv. 7-8, the benediction shifts from physical dangers to spiritual ones. "The LORD will keep you from all evil" (or "May the LORD keep you . . .") could be read in different ways. The word translated as "evil" could refer to personal wickedness, to the harmful results of wrongdoing, or to calamity in general.

We could use protection on all counts, hoping to avoid the temptation to choose evil in our own lives, as well as to escape harm that might come from others' bad actions or from the dangerous vicissitudes of daily life.

A more positive way of affirming God's care is found in the assurance that God "will keep your life." Ancient Hebrew thought did not separate body and soul, as Greek philosophers did. The belief that God would keep one's life included everything related to this life and to whatever lies beyond.

Many people find special comfort in this verse. Even though we shouldn't expect God to step in or send angels to protect us from all harm, we can be confident that God is present with us in all situations, even tragic ones.

The final verse summarizes all that has come before it, a benedictory hope that "the LORD will keep your going out and your coming in from this time on and forevermore" (v. 8).

"Going out and coming in" serves as an idiom for all of life, whether traveling or at home, whether coming or going. The psalmist would not have understood the New Testament concept of heaven, but still trusted God to be both present and protective for as long as time shall last.

Modern readers may share the poet's confident trust, and even more so in the light of the New Testament's similar images of Christ as the Good Shepherd who watches his sheep and doesn't allow any to become lost.

As the psalmist found strength in the multiplied assertions that God is a present "keeper" both day and night, both coming and going, so followers of Jesus may affirm with Paul that "the peace of God, which surpasses all understanding, will guard your hearts and your minds in Christ Jesus" (Phil. 4:7).

God is our keeper: that's a thought worth holding on to.

For reflection: *Can you think of times when you sensed God's presence even though things were going badly or tragedy had struck? Does the promise of God's present care imply that God must protect us from all harm?*

THE HARDEST QUESTION
Is Psalm 121 a promise, or a blessing?

It's easy to misunderstand Psalm 121, because a surface reading of it in most translations seems to promise more than the psalm delivers: Experience tells us that God does not provide the perfect protection the psalm appears to affirm.

One interpretive approach to this conundrum is to recognize that the psalm has characteristics of a blessing or benediction along with a promise: It is a wish for God to provide constant protection as well as an affirmation of God's faithful presence.

One clue to this is found in v. 3, where the verbs might best be translated as a wish rather than a certainty. For most verbs in Hebrew, the imperfect and jussive forms are identical. The imperfect form typically refers to uncompleted action, and depending on context can describe past, present, or future events. The jussive form indicates a wish or command, either "May he give" or a more imperative "Let him give."

While most translations have rendered the verbs as imperfects, giving the entire psalm the character of a promise, the NET regards the verbs in v. 3 as jussives, giving the remainder of the psalm the form of a blessing or benediction.

Consider the memorable Aaronic blessing of Num. 6:24-26: "The LORD bless you and keep you; the LORD make his face to shine upon you, and be gracious to you; the LORD lift up his countenance upon you, and give you peace." The verbs in that text could also be read as either a promise or a wish: "The LORD will bless you" as opposed to "May the LORD bless you." It is the context that clearly suggests blessing over promise.

While Ps. 121:3 appears to be more of a blessing, vv. 4-8 are more like a divine oracle in form, a priestly promise that all will be for good. Oracles were sometimes regarded as certain, especially in prophetic contexts. When uttered by priests, however, oracles could have the sense of a wish.

Following Hannah's vow in 1 Samuel 1, for example, the priest Eli responded: "Go in peace; the God of Israel will grant the petition you have made to him" (NRSV)—or "Go in peace, and may the God of Israel grant the request that you have asked of him" (NET).

Technically, the verb could as easily be translated as "the God of Israel *will* grant the request . . .," but the context suggests that Eli's response is more of a hopeful blessing than a certain promise, though Hannah could have heard it in either sense.

We find a similar situation with Psalm 121. Typical translations give it the appearance of one long promise, but a closer reading suggests that the psalm combines elements of both promise and blessing—a beautiful benediction for believers.

NOTES

[1]Learn more from Amy Cuddy's presentation on "Ted Talks" at http://www.ted.com/talks/amy_cuddy_your_body_language_shapes_who_you_are.html).

[2]"Commentary on Ps 64," on v. 3, in Peter Brown, *Augustine of Hippo: A Biography* (London: Faber, 1967), 315.

Psalm 123

FEELING DOWN, BUT LOOKING UP

To you I lift up my eyes,
O you who are enthroned in the heavens!
—Psalm 123:1

Have you ever felt the cold sting of contempt? Can you remember situations in which others looked down on you, despised you, or called you names? Can you remember how deeply that hurt, especially if it went on and on?

The author of today's text knew that feeling. So did others in whose behalf the psalmist prayed. Psalm 123 is a short, plaintive appeal to God from suffering Hebrews who have been scorned and mistreated by prideful people who act as if they are superior.

How does one express such sorrow in the form of a song? It's not just that things haven't gone their way. The people have been abused and degraded, forced into a place that robbed them of dignity and purpose. They may have felt in danger of losing what little identity they had left. That kind of feeling seems deeper and darker than the blues.

What kind of song could give voice to that kind of pain and pathos that goes beyond the blues, and yet not give up altogether? We don't know what kind of tune or rhythm the ancient psalmist used when he penned this prayer, but if we sang it today I am confident that it would sound like a Negro spiritual.

The dark period in which slavery thrived in America stands as an ignoble blemish on our history. Men and women and children were robbed of their freedom, separated from their families, traded, loaned, and used like any other kind of property.

We wonder how anyone could have survived such abuse. Yet, by strength of will and by human hope and often by faith in God, many did survive, and they left a legacy of courage and determination and shared hope that found its voice in a style of music we speak of as "spirituals." Spirituals possess a haunting style that almost miraculously finds a way to express deep pathos and abiding hope at the same time.

I hear the same thing when I read Psalm 123, and try to imagine how it would have sounded. I think it sounds like a spiritual. ♥

♥ **Psalm 123 as a spiritual:** When I read Psalm 123, I think of v. 1 as a sort of chorus that could be repeated, followed by three verses describing the people's sorrow. I've recast the first verse as an appeal for the people to look up to God, which is what the psalmist is doing—on the people's behalf—in v. 1. I've paraphrased the other verses for rhythm and rhyme, but in a way that expresses the same concerns we find voiced by the biblical text.[1]

(chorus)
Look up to heaven, look up to heaven,
look up to heaven land where God is on his throne. (repeat)

(v. 2)
The eyes of a servant must look to his master,
    the eyes of a handmaid will trust in her mistress,
So we will look to our Lord and God above us,
    Lord have mercy on our souls . . .

(chorus)

(v. 3)
Have mercy upon us, Lord have mercy,
    have mercy upon us, Lord have mercy,
We have been hated, abused and degraded,
    how long will this go on?

(chorus)

(v. 4)
Have mercy upon us, for others have scorned us,
    safe in their power, they look down upon us,
Our hearts overflow with the pain of our sorrow,
    Lord have mercy on our souls . . .

(chorus)

AN UNFAIR WORLD
(vv. 3-4)

Ordinarily, we study a text by starting at the beginning, but with this one, it's best to start with the final two verses and work backward because it is in vv. 3-4 that we find the cause of the people's pain, for which vv. 1-2 is a response.

The psalmist speaks of a life that overflows with the contempt of others (v. 3). The Hebrew term we translate as "contempt" would be pronounced *booz*, surprisingly similar in sound to the modern practice of showing derision to a speaker or athlete with a rain of boos.

The closing verse repeats the thought of v. 3 with only slightly more detail: those who scorn the psalmist are described as "those who are at ease" (NRSV, the NET has "the self-assured") and "the proud."

So, what was the situation in life of these burdened people? The psalm itself offers few clues, certainly not enough to arrive at a firm conclusion. Some scholars envision that the psalm emerged from the exilic period, when many Israelites were forcibly relocated to Babylon and some were pressed into involuntary servitude.

Others imagine a post-exilic setting, as Hebrews newly returned from the exile faced hostile opposition from neighboring peoples as they struggled to regain their standing and re-establish themselves in Jerusalem.

It is just as likely, however, that the psalm could reflect the lot of the many poor people who endured harsh economic conditions and suffered at the hands of their own countrymen. Eighth-century prophets such as Amos, Hosea, Micah, and Isaiah of Jerusalem condemned wealthy Israelites who took advantage of the poor, creating untenable situations in which unpayable debts led to the loss of land, homes, and even personal freedom. If "those who are at ease" in v. 4 is intended to denote wealthy persons who demean their servants or hired help, that might suggest a situation that pitted differing economic classes among the Hebrews.

Sometimes it is to our benefit that we don't know the precise setting of a psalm, for the very ambiguity of it allows the psalm to speak more clearly to our own place in life. The author of this psalm sang of personal suffering, both for himself and for the entire group of worshipers who were with him. They had been badly mistreated. They had been abused and victimized by others who were more powerful. They had been left with no one to call upon except for God.

For reflection: *Can you identify with this kind of song? Have you ever felt mistreated, put down, or humiliated? Few things leave our spirits more bruised than to be shamed, demeaned, or degraded before others. It is not something we forget easily.* ⬇

♥ A bitter memory: The first time I felt the sting of another's contempt was more than 50 years ago, but the memory of it has remained clear when so many other things have been forgotten. While attending my first church youth function as a seventh-grader, I won a prize for being the only youth who could identify the type of fruit used as the model for bells on the high priest's robe.

I correctly answered "pomegranate," and my prize was a brown paper bag containing an actual pomegranate—something most of us had never seen. I felt proud to have known the answer, and was surprisingly excited to own a genuine biblical fruit.

Before the night was over, however, a young bully snatched the bag from the table, ran outside, and stomped on it. When my father came to pick me up, I was cradling the soggy remains of my pomegranate, crying bitter seventh-grade tears, failing to understand how or why anyone could be so mean.

It was a Psalm 123 moment.

For reflection: We all have to learn, at some point, that life isn't always fair. We live in a world where people are often mistreated, and being a Christian does not protect us from it. Does that mean that God doesn't care?

ACTING AND REACTING
(vv. 1-2)

If public embarrassment or criticism should come as no surprise, then what do we do when it comes? How do we react when others hurt us? Our first reaction may be to strike back. Children, for example, learn the art of name calling early on, and sometimes it takes a while to grow out of it.

Belittling others is a natural way of reacting when others treat us badly. But God's people are called to live a different kind of life, to set a different kind of example. We are not only to *act* like God's people, but also to *react* like God's people.

The author of Psalm 123 dealt with adversity by trusting in God for personal strength to endure, and by leaving any vengeance in the hands of God. The psalmist did not speak harm to the hurtful, but cried in hope to the helpful, trusting in God for mercy and grace to replace the scorn and contempt that filled his soul.

In v. 1, the writer speaks as an individual, but with v. 2 it becomes evident that he or she is praying on behalf of a beleaguered people. In addressing God as "you who are enthroned in the heavens," the supplicant acknowledges that God alone is sovereign—thus throwing a spotlight on the errant assumption of those who think they are in a position to heap scorn upon others.

With v. 2, the author employs the central metaphor in the psalm, likening the suffering people's situation to that of servants who have no power of their own, but must look to the hand of their master for protection. In Hebrew thought, "hand" is often used as a metaphor for power, especially of God (e.g. Exod. 32:11; Deut. 2:15; Ps. 18:35, 21:8, 31:15, 63:8, among many others).

The first two couplets of v. 2 are in synonymous parallel, a common poetic style in which the second line echoes the thought of the verse. Here, the poet's reference to male servants in the first line and a female servant in the next "conveys a sense of inclusiveness: Everyone in this community, man and woman, looks urgently to God for a sign of grace."[2]

The psalmist recognizes that the only hope for the oppressed is found in God: While proud humans show only contempt, the downtrodden cry out to God "until he has mercy upon us" (v. 4).

When Jesus talked to his disciples about dealing with hurtful people, he said "I say to you that listen: love your enemies, do good to those who hate you, bless those who curse you, pray for those who abuse you" (Luke 6:27-28).

Jesus took the psalmist's approach, but he took it a step further. The world we inhabit lives by the rule of an eye for an eye, a tooth for a tooth, a push for a push, and a name for a name. But Jesus tells us to follow a different road. He tells us to take all the hurt that others pour out, and turn it into something positive. He calls us to be transformers, people who literally turn evil into good.

Jesus took the worst this world could throw at him, and turned it into the best thing that could be done for the world. He

⇓ A lovely bunch of coconuts: I don't know the original source of this slightly whimsical parable, but it illustrates the notion that one can transform harm into good:

Perhaps you have heard the story of a man who was walking through the jungle when a monkey high up in a palm tree threw a young coconut and hit him square on the head.

The man fell to the earth for a minute, then thought, "I'm thirsty." So he used his machete to lop off the top of the coconut, and drank the cool, sweet coconut water that was inside.

"Ah," he said, "Now I'm hungry!" So he split the coconut and ate the delicious white fruit that lined the shell.

"Now," he thought, "I could use a new spoon and fork." So he took his knife and whittled the coconut shell into some very useful utensils.

He then looked up into the tree, and shouted "Thank you, Mr. Monkey. I appreciate your criticism!"

> ⚓ **Transformers:** I am convinced that we truly can be transformers. Consider the promise of Rom. 8:28—"We know that all things work together for good for those who love God, who are called according to his purpose." This verse does not say that all things are good or that all things happen according to God's purpose, but it does suggest that those who love God can work together to see something good emerge even from the most awful of tragedies.
>
> I have seen it happen in my life, and perhaps you have, too. Think about situations in which you have seen something good come out of pain, struggle, or sorrow. There may be more than you realize.

challenges us to follow his example, to be transformers, to make our world a better place. ⚓

The world is not a fair place to live, and life is often hard. But even when people mistreat us, when life does not seem fair, we can look up to heaven, we can trust in God's care, we can follow Christ's example, we can transform evil into good. When we recognize that happening, it may be the greatest miracle we will ever see.

> **For reflection:** *Can you recall a time when you were able to offer kindness to someone who was rude or hurtful to you? Did it make a difference? If so, how?*

THE HARDEST QUESTION
What is a "song of ascent"?

Psalm 123 is fairly straightforward, and the thorniest question might have to do with the superscription, a note added to the psalm by a later editor. The psalm is called a "song of ascent." Fifteen of the psalms (120-134) bear this label. Scholars have advanced a number of conjectures about what the title means, but none have been conclusive.

Some suggest that a "song of ascent" began on a low note and ascended to a higher one, which seems unlikely. Others guess that it is intended to elevate God, but the content of the so-labeled psalms are no more likely to praise God than the others.

It is said that there were 15 semi-circular steps ascending from the outer to the inner courtyard of the temple, so some suppose the 15 songs of ascents were recited on those steps.

Rabbi Naftali Silberberg relates a curious old rabbinic tale that during construction of a channel on the temple mount, a flood came up from the deep and threatened the earth. To abate it, David wrote God's name on a pottery shard and threw it into the depths, whereupon the water receded 16,000 cubits, leaving the earth too dry (a cubit is about 18 inches). David then sang the 15 songs of ascent, causing the water to rise 15,000 cubits so it was closer to the earth's surface.[3]

A more likely view is that the songs of ascent were pilgrim songs typically sung by those who came to worship at the temple during the three annual feasts or at other times. Since Jerusalem is on a high hill, one cannot enter the city without ascending from one of the surrounding valleys.

There is a metaphorical element, too. In the Bible, whenever someone travels to Jerusalem, they "go up" to Jerusalem. In addition to being physically elevated, Jerusalem was the religious, political, and economic heart of the nation, so one always "went up" to it.

Perhaps we can imagine a group of suffering pilgrims who make their way to Jerusalem, intending to bring their case before God and plead for vindication. Like slaves who sing haunting but hopeful spirituals as they work, pilgrims might have sung these songs as they climbed into the city where God was thought to dwell.

NOTES

[1]A video version of the song can be found at http://www.nurturingfaith.net/adult-archives/category/november-2011. A free digital copy of sheet music for the song, including four-part harmonies composed by Georgeanne Murdock, can be obtained by contacting the author at cartledge@baptiststoday.org.

[2]Robert Alter, *The Book of Psalms: A Translation with Commentary* (New York: Norton & Co., 2007), 441.

[3]See http://www.chabad.org/library/article_cdo/aid/655450/jewish/What-is-a-Song-of-Ascents.htm.

Psalm 130

CAN I HAVE A LITTLE HOPE?

If you, O LORD, should mark iniquities,
Lord, who could stand?
—Psalm 130:3

Have you ever felt totally guilty before God, overwhelmed by a sense of sin and failure, longing for the blessed release of forgiveness? You would not be the first: Psalm 130 is the story of a person who felt just that way.

This psalm is often read in Christian worship during the season of Lent, a seven-week period of penitence preceding Easter. During Lent, believers are challenged to take a close look at their lives, to identify areas in which they have fallen short of God's desire, and to seek a new start through asking forgiveness and turning away from their sins. ☿

> ☿ **Deep words:** An old Christian tradition gave to Psalm 130 the title *De Profundis* ("out of the depths"), from the opening two words in the Latin Vulgate translation. The psalm's penitent theme is so memorable and timeless that the title has been adopted by a variety of literary and musical works (including a ballet and a sonata), as well as films.[1]

Psalm 130 is known in church tradition as *De Profundis,* Latin for "out of the depths," the first words. It is the sixth of seven "penitential psalms" designated by the early church to be recited on Ash Wednesday (the others are 6, 32, 38, 51, 102, and 143) and promoted as appropriate for any time of confession and repentance.

A PENITENT PRAYER
(vv. 1-4)

The psalm's designation as a "song of ascent" goes back to Jewish tradition and some of our earliest manuscripts. ☿ The psalm appears to have originated as a testimony

⬓ **Songs of ascent:** Fifteen of the psalms (120-134) bear this label. Most scholars assume that the songs of ascent were pilgrim songs typically sung by those who came to worship at the temple during the three annual feasts or at other times. Since Jerusalem is on a high hill, one cannot enter the city without ascending from one of the surrounding valleys.

The ancient steps in the picture below were uncovered below the southern wall of the Temple Mount in Jerusalem. From here, pilgrims ascended to one of several gates that led to stairways accessing the temple courts.

of an individual's private devotion, but it could also have found a place in worship as a corporate prayer of penitence. ⬓

The psalmist appears to be deeply troubled by his failures, but gives no clue as to the nature of his sin. We don't know if he was under conviction about a particularly egregious error, or if more frequent foibles had mounted up. Whatever the case, he had a sense of being in deep water, caught up in the chaos of sin and struggling to keep his head above water, knowing that God was his only hope: "Out of the depths I cry to you, O LORD" (v. 1).

The word translated as "depths" could possibly refer to the abode of the dead in the depths of the earth, or to the deep waters of the ungoverned sea, which represented chaos to the ancients. Hebrew has several words that

⬓ **Similar psalms:** Mitchell Dahood notes that Psalm 130 bears several similarities to Psalm 86, which is considered a royal psalm, suggesting that the individual whose lament and testimony are recorded here was to be identified as a king of Israel. If that is the case, the psalm would date to the period before the Babylonian exile.

Both Psalm 130 (vv. 2, 3, 6) and Psalm 86 (vv. 3, 5, 8, 12, 15) address God as Adonai, typically translated as "Lord" (with upper and lower case letters, as opposed to the personal divine name Yahweh or Yah, usually rendered as "LORD.")

Both psalms also use the phrase translated as "voice of my supplications" (130:2, 86:6). And a rare noun for "forgiveness" used in 130:4 appears in 86:5 as an adjectival form, meaning "forgiving."[2]

Other scholars argue that linguistic features of the psalm are more typical of the later, post-exilic period.

convey the sense of something deep, and the one used here often appears in negative circumstances: for those who hide the plans "deeply" from Yahweh (Isa. 29:15), or who are urged to hide from Yahweh in the "depths" of Dedan (Jer. 49:8). Hos. 5:2 appears to speak of those who are "deep" in depravity.

It's not surprising, then, that the psalmist would use this word to describe the extent of his shortcomings.

Perhaps you can remember feeling overwhelmed by failure, emotionally at sea, floundering for a footing. You may have sought the ear of a friend or counselor—or you may have prayed to God, as the psalmist did (v. 2).

> ⬥ **LORD, and Lord:** Note this psalm's characteristic pairing of two different names for God, the personal name Yahweh (or Yah, translated LORD), and the more generic term Adonai, translated as "Lord." At the end of v. 1 and the beginning of v. 2, they come together: "I cry to you, Yahweh: Adonai, hear my voice!" In v. 3, we find "If you kept records of sin, Yah–Adonai, who could stand?" The pair appears again in vv. 5-6, with "I wait for Yahweh" in v. 5 and "my soul (waits) for Adonai" in v. 6.

Fully aware of his faults—and of the pervasive nature of sin in human life—the poet sought divine mercy rather than judgment. To his plea for mercy, the psalmist adds a rational appeal: "If you, O LORD, should mark iniquities, Lord, who could stand?" (v. 3). ⬥

The word translated as "mark" is also used to mean "watch," "guard," or "keep." In essence, the psalmist is saying that if God kept score and judged our errors accordingly, no one would be left standing.

Many believers hold to the view of a judgmental God who keeps meticulous records of wrongdoing. Some teachers or preachers take an almost perverse delight in drawing a picture of judgment day in which every sin would be revealed for all the world to see (1 Cor. 4:5 is sometimes cited as support for this view).

The psalmist understood, however, that God has better things to do than compile an individual encyclopedia of failures for every person on earth. He understood that God is gracious and forgiving, and that forgiveness means—well, forgiveness.

If we truly forgive someone of hurting us, there's no need to hold on to the offense or remind them of it or keep records for future reference. If God kept a daily tally and punished us for every sin, few of us would survive for very long.

Rather, the poet affirmed God's gracious nature: "But there is forgiveness with you, so that you may be revered" (v. 4).

For reflection: *Think about this: What good would it do for God to wipe out all who sin and have no one left with whom to fellowship or for whom to have hopes and dreams? How could God be praised if no one was left to sing hallelujahs? If anyone is to worship and pay reverence to God, it must be sinners, because there is no other type of person. And if sinners are to live and serve God, it must be because God is gracious and willing to forgive. When you ask God for forgiveness, are you asking for what you deserve, or for grace?*

Many people—both believers and unbelievers—have difficulty in forgiving other people, or even forgiving themselves. They keep a running tally of wrongs that amounts to a heavy load of misery. To find the joy that God wants for us, we must learn to forgive and to be forgiven, to stop keeping score and find true freedom.

A LONGING HOPE
(vv. 5-6)

Believing that God is gracious and actually experiencing forgiveness are two different things. Having confessed his sins and expressed confidence in God's forgiving nature, the psalmist waited for a sign of absolution. Verse 5 consists of three brief clauses: "I wait for the LORD, my soul waits, and in his word I hope."

A surface reading of this verse might lead some to think "in his word I hope" is a reference to trusting in the Bible, but that is a misuse of scripture, taking a word out of one context and inserting it into another. The psalmist had no Bible, for most of it had not yet been written or become widely known. In Old Testament contexts such as this one, terms such as "his word" or "the word of God" refer to a direct message from God, usually delivered as an oracle through a prophet or priest who spoke in God's behalf.

The preposition before "his word" usually means "to" or "for" rather than "in." The psalmist is voicing a longing for a word from God to indicate that his sins have been forgiven. The poet may have hoped for something as objective as a priestly oracle declaring that God had heard his prayer and granted clemency. Or, he may have sought a more subjective sense of inner peace and release through a divine response.

The verb for "waits" does not appear in v. 6, as in many translations. The line poetically carries forward the sense of hope and longing from the previous verse, which ends with "I hope . . ." and is followed by " . . . my soul, more than watchers for the morning, watchers for the morning."

"Watchers for the morning" could refer to guards or others appointed to keep watch through the night, but also echoes the sense of someone who suffers deep anxiety or guilt and cannot sleep. The psalmist longs for God's forgiveness even more keenly than an insomniac or troubled person watches through the night, waiting for the light of day. ✒

For reflection: *Have you ever lost sleep because of a troubled spirit that left you staring at a dark ceiling and longing for the dawn? What had to happen before you found rest again?*

A RELIEVED TESTIMONY
(vv. 7-8)

With vv. 7-8, the psalm turns from speaking *to* God (vv. 1-4) and speaking *about* God (vv. 5-6) to speaking *for* God, urging the people of Israel to seek God and find the same sense of forgiveness that he apparently received. ✒

Some interpreters see vv. 7-8 as spoken by a priest or prophet who exhorts the congregation to follow the example of the person who speaks in vv. 1-6 and turn to God so they may also experience forgiveness and renewed faith.

Whoever the speaker might be, v. 5 and v. 7 both stress the importance of hope. There is a sense in which we all live on hope. We awake each morning hoping for a good day. We enter relationships hoping to find love and companionship. We hope that our lives might have some

✒ **Intentional, or not?:** As noted in the lesson, a literal reading of v. 6 could be "my soul (waits) for the Lord, more than the watchers of the morning, watchers of the morning."

Many early commentators argued that the second "watchers of the morning" should be deleted as the error of a copyist who accidentally wrote the same words twice, a mistake known as dittography.

More recent scholars, however, have argued that the repetition is intentional, used for effect to indicate the depth of the psalmist's longing for a sense of release from sin.

What do you think?

✒ **Original, or added?**
Some older commentaries suggest that vv. 7-8, which address Israel rather than God, were not original to the psalm, but added when it came to be used in worship.

Scholars who focus on literary characteristics of the psalm are more likely to argue that the verses reflect the same theological theme and are structurally related to earlier parts of the psalm.

What do you think?

significance and that our children will appreciate us. We hope to stay healthy and to live a long time.

Furthermore, we hope for a meaningful existence that extends beyond this earthly life, though we have no human means of making that happen or any proof that it will. The basis for such a hope is found in the promises of a dependably loving and forgiving God. Just as the psalmist called on Israel to "hope in the LORD," hope is what keeps us going.

The closing verses of the psalm are addressed to Israel, but God's promise of forgiveness extends far beyond the covenant people of the Old Testament. The Hebrew Bible depicts God as gracious to all who repent, with the book of Jonah being a prime example of God's willingness to forgive the wicked people of Ninevah, even when a prophet thought they didn't deserve it.

Viewing the text through the lens of the New Testament, we are reminded that God offers grace to "whosoever" (John 3:16), and that "If we confess our sins, he who is faithful and just will forgive us our sins and cleanse us from all unrighteousness" (1 John 1:9).

All of us know what it is like to fall short of God's expectations. Some of us have known or may now know the psalmist's feeling of drowning in failure. Even from those chaotic depths—and perhaps, especially from the depths—we can learn from the psalmist to trust in God's steadfast love and find the redemption we crave.

May it be so.

For reflection: *Chaos. Failure. Loss. Are these terms familiar to you? Can you identify with the feeling of being overwhelmed, drowning in sorrow or swamped by more than you could do? How did you get your head back above water? Did God have anything to do with it?*

THE HARDEST QUESTION
Does God keep score?

Many people, both in the church and without, hold to a belief that God keeps a record of our good and bad deeds, and will one day judge whether we get into heaven by weighing the good against the bad. This is not a biblical teaching. The psalms and prophets speak of the wicked being unable to stand in the judgment (Pss. 1:5, 9:16; Mic. 7:9; Hab. 1:2; Mal. 3:5), but for the Hebrews God's judgment could take place on earth at any time rather than as a prelude to eternity: the New Testament concept of eternal life in heaven had not yet developed.

Several New Testament passages suggest that all will give an account of themselves at the judgment, with eternity in the balance (Matt. 12:36, Rom. 2:5, 2 Cor. 4:5, 1 Pet. 4:5, among others). This does not mean that God keeps a record of every wrong, however, or will replay our sins for all to see. Can you imagine how long that would take, or a more discouraging way to start eternity?

The Bible consistently holds that God is forgiving, and forgiveness is antithetical to keeping score. When we repent of our sins and seek God's forgiveness, whatever record we may have accumulated is wiped clean. That's what forgiveness means. Isaiah, looking to the future and speaking for God, wrote: "I, I am He who blots out your transgressions for my own sake, and I will not remember your sins" (Isa. 43:25).

Jeremiah spoke of a God who "will remember their iniquity and punish their sins" (speaking of Israel, Jer. 14:10), but also of a time when everyone would know the Lord, "for I will forgive their iniquity, and remember their sin no more" (Jer. 31:34).

Jesus had a lot to say about forgiveness as well as the importance of forgiving others. At the Last Supper he said, "This is the blood of the covenant, which is poured out for many for the forgiveness of sins" (Matt. 26:28). Paul spoke of how "God made you alive together with him, when he forgave us all our trespasses" (Col. 2:13). The writer of 1 John declared: "If we confess our sins, he who is faithful and just will forgive us our sins and cleanse us from all unrighteousness" (1:9).

If God kept a record of every sin and expected us to outweigh them with good, none of us could be saved. The author of Psalm 130 knew this: "If you, O LORD, should mark iniquities, Lord, who could stand?" But he also believed that God is gracious: "But there is forgiveness with you, so that you may be revered" (Ps. 130:3-4).

To say that God forgives and does not remember our sins does not mean the acts are no longer present in the divine memory, but that God no longer holds them against us. Likewise, we are challenged to forgive others when they do us wrong. We may still recall how someone offended us, but we no longer hold it against them: it no longer holds any weight.

If God kept score as we are prone to do, we would be like a basketball team that saw every player foul out before the end of the first half, or like a baseball team that found itself 100 runs behind in the first inning. We would be hopeless and helpless.

God relates to us on the basis of steadfast love and a redeeming grace that exceeds our comprehension. No matter what we have done or how often we have done it, God is willing to forgive our sins and wipe the slate clean and keep us in the game.

How grateful we can be that God does not keep score.

NOTES

[1] For a list, see http://en.wikipedia.org/wiki/De_Profundis.

[2] Mitchell Dahood, *Psalms III:1-1-150*, Anchor Bible, vol. 17A (New York: Doubleday, 1970), 235.

AFTERWORD

The psalms of lament, written thousands of years ago, remind us that sin and suffering are an inevitable part of the human condition, but not the inevitable end of the story. The psalmists knew that the reality of God brings the promise of hope, and they found a broad range of ways to express both personal need and spiritual hope.

The psalms we have considered in these lessons begin and end with penitence, a necessary precursor for those who know they have fallen short but look to God for forgiveness or deliverance. Psalm 25 is the prayer of an individual who seeks divine mercy to blot out past iniquity, while Psalm 130 records not only a prayer for pardon, but also the grateful testimony of one who feels forgiven.

The people of Israel knew stubbornness as well as penitence, however. Psalm 78 imagines how God must sing the blues over a recalcitrant people who persistently turn away, while Psalm 80 is a prayer for God to turn toward the weak nation with the light of divine grace.

Psalms of lament deal with more than penitence, however. We know from experience that hard things come to all of us, and the suffering we experience may seem to have no meaning. Psalm 121 offers an encouraging testimony of hope from one sufferer who looked to God as the source of deliverance and care. Psalm 123 reverberates with the haunting cry of a people who have been abused without cause, but who trust in God nevertheless.

In these psalms we find people who have been broken down but have not given up. As we walk our own life's journey, we may experience failure that comes from within or injustice that comes from without. The psalmists remind us that we are not alone in this. From the stance of our own wrongdoing, we may cry for forgiveness and be assured of pardon. From the depths of our suffering or sorrow, when it seems that God is our only hope, we can remember that God truly *is* our hope.

And for that we can be eternally grateful.

CPSIA information can be obtained at www.ICGtesting.com
Printed in the USA
LVOW04s1310040515

437128LV00002BA/4/P